Kara's PARTY IDEAS

KARA ALLEN

Kara's PARTY IDEAS

CD with PRINTABLE invites and party decor INCLUDED

FRONT TABLE BOOKS | SPRINGVILLE, UTAH

ISBN: 978-1-4621-1104-6 (paperback edition)
ISBN: 978-1-4621-1157-2 (hardback edition)

Published by Front Table Books, an imprint of Cedar Fort, Inc., 2373 W. 700 S., Springville, UT 84663
Distributed by Cedar Fort, Inc., www.cedarfort.com

Library of Congress Cataloging-in-Publication data on file

Cover and page design by Erica Dixon
Cover design © 2012 by Lyle Mortimer
Edited by Michelle Stoll

Printed in Hong Kong

10 9 8 7 6 5 4 3 2

Printed on neutralized paper

"It's not enough to have a dream unless I'm willing to pursue it. It's not enough to know what's right unless I'm strong enough to do it. It's not enough to join the crowd, to be acknowledged and accepted. I must be true to my ideals, even if I'm left out and rejected. It's not enough to learn the truth unless I also learn to live it. It's not enough to reach for love unless I care enough to give it." —Anonymous

The above quote was on my dresser from the time I was young to the day I left for college. I read it over and over and have thought about those words time and time again. I have always been the kind of person who—instead of asking "why?"—asks "why not?" This book has been a dream of mine for a very long time. I believe in dreaming. I believe in doing everything in your power to make your dreams come true.

I dedicate this book to Sarah Miskin. Thank you for being that friend next to me all those summer nights in the backyard on the trampoline when we were just girls. I'll never forget gazing up at the stars and talking late into the night about what we were going to do in life. I know that I always promised I would publish a song for you, but until then, I hope this will do. Maybe you did know something when you said I would be a writer. This definitely isn't a novel, and I know you meant a songwriter, but this is my song for you, Sarah. I love you and always will.

Contents

21

31

39
Cream

47

PRINCESS BIRTHDAY PARTY

Photography by Valerie Hart Photography

www.ValerieHartPhotography.com

What little girl doesn't dream of being a princess? Nestled in a gorgeous blooming orchard, this Princess Birthday Party for a beautiful eight-year-old girl was nothing but dreamy!

THE SECOND I LEARNED there was an orchard near my home that was about to bloom, I knew it would be the perfect setting for the princess party I was planning. The white and pink apricot blossoms created a natural backdrop that I knew I could never come close to creating anywhere else.

THE INVITATION for this party was unique because it was an actual party hat! The invitation template (included on the CD) was printed on pink floral cardstock, shaped into a hat, and then embellished with a tulle train, pink ruffle ribbon, and shiny silver cording.

THE GUESTS were asked to come to the party dressed in white, fancy "princess attire." They looked absolutely adorable! The smile on each girl's face was priceless when they arrived and had a white lace crown (which I made with lace, ribbon, and fabric stiffener) pinned to her hair and a candy bracelet with a princess crown charm placed on her wrist.

I SET UP THE MAIN TABLE for the party in the middle of one of the orchard rows. I first put a white-and-pink floral tablecloth on the table and then topped it with a gathered, silky pink fabric that coordinated with the birthday girl's dress.

IN THE TREES SURROUNDING THE TABLE, I hung tulle poms and carnation pomander balls. Around the table were child-sized white, wooden chairs. Hanging from the back of each chair were white eyelet favor cones filled with pink Sixlet® candies. The focal point of the main party table was the incredible Princess Carriage cake, created by Marcee Kitchen of Dippidee. The detail of the cake was absolutely amazing! It demanded attention from its spot on the top tier of a sparkly chandelier-style cake and cupcake stand. White vanilla-flavored cupcakes topped with princess crown candleholders were sitting on each of the lower pedestals of the stand. One cupcake was topped with a fondant princess slipper and pillow to match the cake.

AT EACH PLACE SETTING on the main table was an ornate white plate topped with a round pink hobnail saucer. A crystal-tipped princess wand and a sparkling crown were on each plate. I set out clear glass teacups at each place to use for drinking glasses. For decoration, I put miniature white ceramic topiaries next to each glass. To the side of each plate was a delicate white vase filled with pink carnations, baby's breath, a star-tipped wand, and a white chocolate–covered Oreo® pop, made by Marcee of Dippidee. Princess castle cupcake holders from my shop were also placed at each setting. Atop the castles were bite-sized shortbread cookies from Dippidee, topped with a high swirl of white frosting and pink flag picks. On the four corners of the table were miniature silver wire baskets filled with puffy vanilla meringues. Small princess castle banks were also set out on the table amongst the decor.

TO THE RIGHT OF THE MAIN TABLE (and underneath an apricot tree with low-hanging branches), I placed a white, ornate wooden nightstand. I love using various furniture pieces in my parties! The nightstand—with its intricate knobs and design—was a perfect fit for the delicate princess theme. I painted a metal chandelier pink and hung it from a tree branch directly above the nightstand. I also hung another pink tulle pom to the side of the nightstand for added charm. Atop the nightstand was a picture of Brindee, the beautiful birthday girl. On one side of the delicate frame was a small apothecary jar filled with pearls, and on the other was a three-tiered pastry stand holding beautiful ribbon cookies made by Dippidee. I set out a princess crown–shaped dish and pink favor boxes across the front of the nightstand. A pink-and-white vintage ice cream parlor chair (a great find from an antique shop) was placed next to the nightstand.

BEHIND THE MAIN TABLE was an enchanting vintage baby doll carriage (a thrift store find), which was used to hold the birthday gifts. To the left of the main table (and nestled at the base of another apricot tree) was a small, pink wooden table, which held a wooden princess castle dollhouse. I used the castle to display the remaining sweets. White eyelet tins were at the front, inside the "courtyard area." In one tin were pink Sixlet® candies and exquisite Princess Carriage Cake Pops from Autumn Lynn's Chocolate Sins' Etsy shop. In the other tin were plastic candy tubes from my shop, filled with white iridescent gumballs.

PLACED INSIDE WINDOWS, on verandas, and on small balconies were mini vanilla cream pies, small white lace cakes, and clear glass dishes filled with round, candy-coated chocolate mints.

DURING THE PARTY, the little "princesses" made necklaces with princess carriage charms and pink silk ribbon. The necklaces were a simple craft for the girls and were the perfect accessory to their princess attire. The girls also used bubble wands and played games with pink and white balloons.

Do you want to re-create this party?

Combined with the templates on the CD and the party details in this chapter, the list below will give you everything you need to get started!

Invitation—Included on CD
Silver princess crowns, pink favor boxes, ribbon, princess carriage charms, candy bracelets, hanging favor cones, lace, crown candle holders, castle cupcake holders, chandelier cake stand, flag cupcake toppers, cupcake wrappers, princess wands, miniature silver spoons & forks, plastic candy tubes, pink Sixlets®, balloons, gumballs, princess gloves, candy-coated chocolate mints—Kara's Party Shop (www.KarasPartyIdeas.com/Shop)
Princess Carriage cake pops—Autumn Lynn's Chocolate Sins online shop (www.etsy.com/shop/AutumnLynnsSins)
Princess Carriage cake, white lace cookies, frosted shortbread cookies, mini vanilla cream pies, cupcakes, white chocolate–covered Oreo® pops—Marcee Kitchen of Dippidee (www.Dippidee.com)
Pink fabric (used for tablecloth), princess castle banks, hanging chandelier—Hobby Lobby
Princess castle dollhouse—Amazon.com

HAPPY
BIRTHDAY
25¢
Enjoy
Coca-Cola

GUMBALL PARTY

Photography by Lyndsey Fagerlund

www.LyndseyFagerlund.com

Bubblegum, bubblegum in a dish, how many gumballs do you wish? This gumball party is full of color and fun! What child wouldn't be thrilled to enter a party held in a room full of bubblegum?

I CREATED THIS PARTY at the request of HGTV. They contacted me looking for a fresh idea to use in an online party feature. I chose a gumball theme because I wanted the party to be something that any child would adore, boys and girls alike. While planning the party, I pictured a vintage gumball machine standing in an old-fashioned soda shoppe. So I decided to give the event a 1950s feel with a red and aqua color scheme, complimented by all of the colors of the rainbow.

I FOUND SOME ADORABLE gumball machine–shaped cookies online and just couldn't resist making them the first purchase for the party!

I ALSO FOUND THE MOST PERFECT red and silver diner-style table that I knew I had to have for the main display. Later, I searched online to find a printable birthday banner and party hats that I could download and print at home. Printables add cute customization to any party at a reasonable price. The process is easy: Find the printable design that works best for the party (there are hundreds of Etsy shops that sell a huge assortment of designs), then just purchase, download, and print! Voila!

SOME OF THE MAIN PARTY ELEMENTS are ready in a snap, without a lot of money, crafting, or searching required. Printables similar to the ones used for this party are found on the included CD.

TO CREATE THE "HAPPY BIRTHDAY" banner, I attached the blue-and-red striped pennant printables onto ruffled red crepe paper. To ruffle the crepe paper, I ran a long strand of it through my sewing machine with the tension set to "loose," sewing a rather sloppy line down the middle.

ONCE FINISHED, I pulled on the thread at one end to create the ruffle. I also glued red pom-poms to the bottom corner of each pennant. To add a little pizzazz to the printable party hats, I attached crepe-paper fringe to the tops and bottoms using hot glue.

THE FRINGE was made in a similar manner to the "Happy Birthday" banner ruffle. I layered four long strips of crepe paper and, using a regular stitch, sewed a straight line all the way up the center of the four-ply strip. I then made small cuts on either side of the sewn line, being careful not to cut into the center. I then separated all of the layers of cut pieces to create the fringe look.

A BIRTHDAY WOULDN'T BE COMPLETE without cupcakes! The only trick was to make sure that even the cupcakes in this party incorporated the bubblegum theme and still added to the soda shoppe feel. Dainty "cherries" on top of the white frosted cupcakes were actually red gumballs! The vintage-style blue and white polka-dot cupcake liners completed the effect.

THE GUMBALL MACHINE–SHAPED cake pops were definitely a favorite! They were actually pretty easy to make! Simply crumble up a cake, combine it with frosting, and chill for two hours. Then mold a flattened cylindrical shape to create the gumball machine base and cover it in red candy melt. Next, insert a long sucker stick through each shape (make sure you insert it all the way through the red base shape so there's room at the top for it to hold the round part of the gumball machine as well). Use a small toothpick and white candy melt to draw a gumball opening in the center of the base. Then cover chilled cake balls (or doughnut holes!) in white candy melt and slide them in place above the red base. Quickly add rainbow sprinkles to the white chocolate candy melt before it dries! Finally, top off the machine with a flat round red candy (I used a "Spree").

I CREATED A BASE FOR THE CAKE POPS by drilling holes in a darling miniature suitcase, which I filled with Styrofoam to add extra strength.

I FOUND SOME OLD-FASHIONED COCA-COLA® crates at a consignment shop and knew they would be a perfect base for a gumball jar display. To make the display, I separated medium-sized gumballs according to their colors and put each uniform group of gumballs into a small, glass jar. I then lined up the filled jars across the bottoms of the staggered, flipped-over crates.

THE TALL, DAZZLING GUMBALL MACHINE in the center of the table was actually a cake! It was brilliantly decorated by Marcee Kitchen of Dippidee. The only part of the cake that wasn't edible was the glass top, which was actually a bowl turned upside-down.

FROM AN ONLINE ETSY SHOP, I ordered white chocolate–covered Oreos® adorned with bold red and pink polka dots made with cocoa butter. They were placed on an aqua blue scaloped plate to round out the playful look.

ON THE MAIN TABLE, I displayed miniature gumball machines on top of blue polka-dot fabric that had red rickrack sewn to the edges. I also tied a polka-dot ribbon to each mini machine. Adding ribbon to party elements is an easy and inexpensive way to bring color and detail to any party.

I TOOK A SIMPLE APPROACH to the drink and activity station. I used a second diner-style table (found online) that fit right in with the 1950s ambiance. The felt polka-dot banner hanging on the wall was an easy, inexpensive DIY decoration that added colorful detail. I made the banner by cutting various sizes of circles out of felt and sewing them together in a line using a sewing machine.

I USED MASON JARS with stamped lids as drinking glasses and inserted red and white paper straws for a classic look. I made "gumball" ice cubes by filling a ball-shaped ice cube tray with red punch. The ice cubes mirrored red gumballs and gave the soda extra flavor.

Bubble gum, Bubble gum in a dish. How many gumballs do you wish?
guess how many
GUMBALLS
are in the jar...

FOR A CHARMING TOUCH, I made a flower bouquet out of gumballs. I hot glued large and small gumballs to plastic Mylar balloon sticks. The sticks have a perfect top that basically held the large center gumball in place (again, with the help of some hot glue). I tied the gumball flowers together with fun ribbon and placed them in a small glass vase. Note: the bouquets definitely aren't edible!

DURING THE PARTY, guests made their own gumball machines (like the ones displayed on the drink table). I went to the craft store to pick up a few simple items to make them. I created the bottom of the machines by painting small terra cotta flower pots red and flipping them upside-down. I glued large, round glass jars on top of the pots, filled the jars with gumballs, and topped them with the terra cotta pot bases, also painted red. I then attached a painted wooden ball to the top so the lid could be removed and replaced more easily. As a final touch, I painted wooden doll pin stands red and glued them to the front of the bases.

AS A FUN ACTIVITY for the younger guests, I placed ribbon wands inside a large jar filled with colorful gumballs. They loved it! These wands correlated with the theme and were very easy to make—simply attach colorful polka-dot ribbons to the top of painted wooden dowels.

FOR ANOTHER PARTY ACTIVITY that all of the guests enjoyed, I filled a jumbo Mason jar with a rainbow of gumballs and had the children try to guess exactly how many gumballs were inside. The person closest to the actual number got to keep the jar! I decorated the guessing table with simple pink bubblegum tape for a pop of color and detail. I placed blue striped "Happy Birthday" treat bags beside the large jar filled with gumballs and ribbon wands, so guests could take any of the delectable treats home with them.

Do you want to re-create this party?

Combined with the templates on the CD and the party details in this chapter, the list below will give you everything you need to get started!

Gumballs, polka-dot cupcake liners, Happy Birthday favor bags, striped paper straws, suitcases, miniature gumball machines, crepe paper, chocolate candy melts, rainbow sprinkles, sucker sticks, ribbon, jars, Mylar balloon sticks, large red balloon, Bubble Tape bubblegum—Kara's Party Shop (www.KarasPartyIdeas.com/Shop)
Bubblegum machine cookies—Batches (www.TheCookieJar.com)
Printable Happy Birthday banner and party hats—Included on CD! Created by Gwynn Wasson Designs (http://www.etsy.com/shop/GwynnWassonDesigns)
Gumball machine cake and cupcakes—Marcee Kitchen of Dippidee (www.Dippidee.com)
Supplies for homemade gumball machine—craft store
Basic cake pop recipe—*101 Gourmet Cake Bites* by Wendy Paul
See this Gumball Party on HGTV—www.hgtv.com/entertaining

POW WOW PARTY

Photography by Valerie Hart Photography

www.ValerieHartPhotography.com

Calling all little American Indians! Head for the mountains and meet us at a birthday pow wow. Slip on your moccasins and get ready for an afternoon of making crafts, eating yummy treats, and playing inside a life-size teepee!

SET AMONG THE INFAMOUS red rock and sand in Snow Canyon, Utah, this pow wow–themed birthday party was one of a kind. In such a gorgeous setting and with such a unique theme, this fourth birthday pow wow could not have been more enjoyable to plan and attend.

The invitations for this party were so fun and easy to make! (The template is included on the CD.) After printing the design onto white cardstock, I cut it out and pasted the pages onto a piece of folded brown cardstock. Then I slid feathers through a slit I made just above the little American Indian's head and secured them with glue. I love how the feathers added dimension and color to the front of each invite.

I SET UP THE MAIN DISPLAY TABLE for this party in a cave-like alcove in the canyon wall. I laid a bright floral patterned piece of fabric, in oranges and blues, over the table. On top of that was a piece of fabric decorated with a geometric design and trimmed with a faux-leather fringe. I then strung a feather banner above the table (made with leather cording, hot glue, and craft feathers).

ALL OF THE FOOD AND TREATS were labeled with tent cards, found on the included CD. I rubbed the stark white cards in the red sand to give them more of a worn-out, muted look. I used a cute little pair of moccasins to hold the wooden forks and spoons; the utensils fit perfectly and looked rustic. In the center of the table were edible teepees that I made by dipping ice cream sugar cones in melted white Wilton Candy Melts® and decorating them with licorice string and various candies. I displayed the cones on a thinly cut wooden slab that resembled a tree stump.

IN FRONT OF THE CONES WERE BROWN, corncob-shaped dishes filled with Boston Baked Bean candies and tan-and-brown swirl lollipops. I used two more of the corncob-shaped dishes to hold the "Corncob Twinkies®." I made these by simply spreading frosting over Twinkies® and placing Reese's Pieces® in rows on top of the frosting. I then wrapped the bottoms of the Twinkies® in cornhusks to enhance the effect. Two large ceramic canoes were also used to hold party treats. One held caramel corn (also placed into corn husks to look like corn on the cob) and the other held cupcakes with dream catcher toppers.

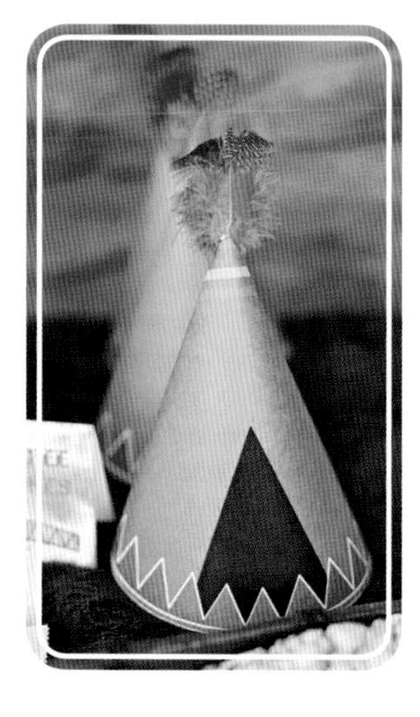

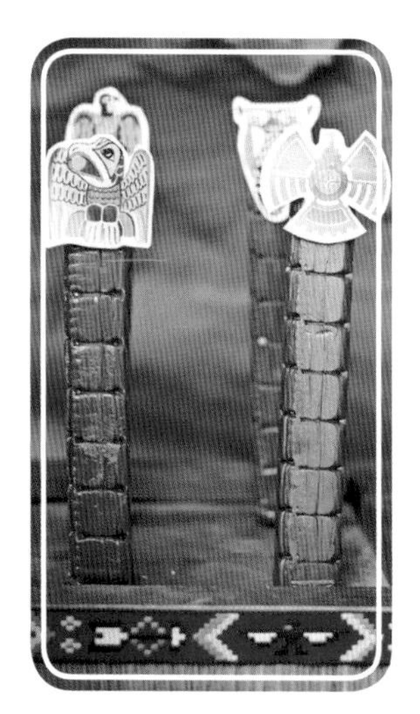
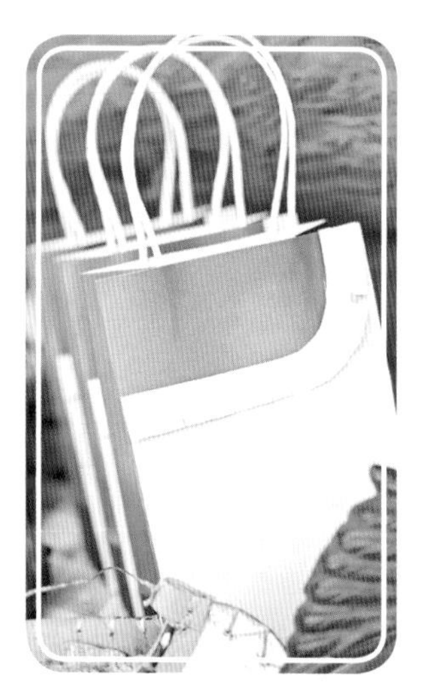

AN OLD TOY DRUM was also used as a cupcake stand. The cupcakes it held were topped with fondant corncob toppers that I ordered online. I also took strands of red licorice and braided them together to make licorice braids. The braids were carefully laid over a smaller toy drum. I had two other canoes, both made out of birchwood, which were used to hold Bugles® snacks (I thought they resembled teepees perfectly) and adorable teepee cake pops that were ordered online from Autumn Lynn's Chocolate Sins. One of my favorite party treats was the "totem poles" that I made with jumbo Tootsie Rolls®! I attached a themed sticker to the top of each upright Tootsie Roll® to complete the effect. On another wooden slab, I placed chocolate marshmallow cookies, topped with fondant American Indian head toppers ordered from www.CookieCovers.net. Cute cactus-shaped sugar cookies, ordered online from www.AllThingsExquisite.com, were displayed behind the chocolate marshmallow cookies. Tall glass jars were filled with candy rocks and small colored beads, which definitely matched the pow wow feel. Large gummy snakes were draped over the corner of the table, held up by an American Indian head bookend wearing a child's bead necklace.

THE PARTY FAVOR SACKS were decorated to look like American Indian dresses. They were simple to make and added so much personality to the table. I cut cream-colored cardstock so that it would cover the face of the brown paper sacks, except for a half-U area at the top (the "neckline" of the dress). After I attached the dress shapes to the bags, I added a fringe across the tops of the "dresses" using the same cream-colored cardstock. Teepee-shaped party hats were made with the printable file found on the CD, and dressed up with ribbon and feathers. Clear glass vases were adorned with children's necklaces, ribbon, and more faux-leather fringe. Inside the vases were toy tomahawks and flutes, which the guests got to play with at the party and take home afterward.

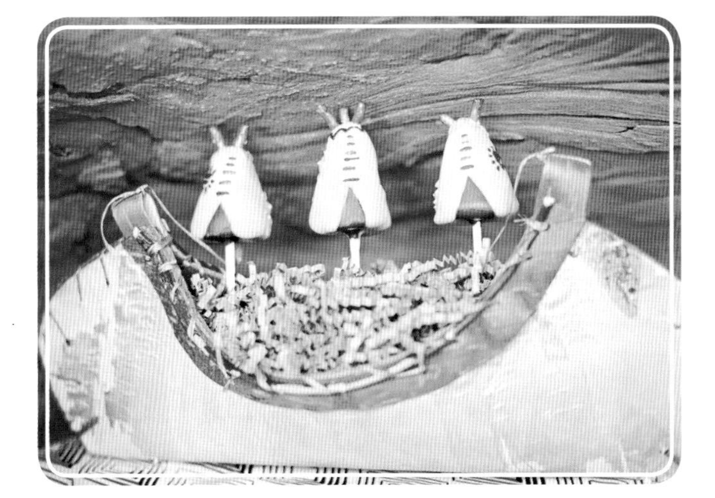

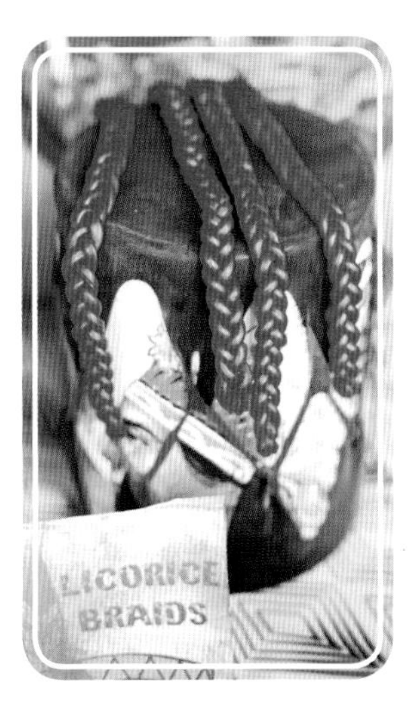

TAFFY
TAFFY
the original old fashioned flat
TAFFY
TAFFY

SET ON TOP of a large red rock was a three-tiered teepee stand holding sweet pow wow–themed cake pops ordered online from Autumn Lynn's Chocolate Sins. The middle tier held little felt drawstring pouches, which were made using a craft kit from my shop. The bottom tier displayed fun American Indian headbands for the kids to wear and take home.

THE FAVORITE PARTY ELEMENT of most of the guests was the child-size teepee! I covered the teepee in various fabric prints to add more depth and color. On the floor of the teepee was an "animal skin" rug that I made using faux fur fabric. I also laid more fabric and fur pieces in front of the teepee to create additional seating.

A FABRIC TRIANGLE PENNANT GARLAND was made with coordinating fabric triangle pieces and leather cording. One side of the banner was strung between the teepee and the rock wall, while the other went from the top of the teepee down to the fun wooden canoe.

FOR THE FIRST PARTY ACTIVITY, the children colored and put together small cardboard teepees using a kit from my shop. Next, they filled glass jars with colored sand, everyone making their own designs. They also cut out cute American Indian paper banners, a download from Happy Paper Hearts. Small bows and arrows and little American Indian dolls were also given to each child to play with throughout the party and take home afterward.

Do you want to re-create this party?

Combined with the templates on the CD and the party details in this chapter, the list below will give you everything you need to get started!

Invitations, food label tent cards, teepee party hats—Templates included on CD
American Indian necklaces, gummy snakes, paper sacks, toy tomahawks, dream catchers, pouch craft kit, teepee craft kit, feathers, glass jars, rock candy, wooden utensils, colored sand, sucker sticks, Wilton Candy Melts®, baker's twine, paper shred, scrapbook paper, paper bags, American Indian headbands—Kara's Party Shop (www.KarasPartyIdeas.com/Shop)
American Indian cake pops—Autumn Lynn's Chocolate Sin's online shop (www.etsy.com/shop/AutumnLynnsSins)
Ceramic canoes, American Indian head bookends—Hobby Lobby
American Indian paper banner—Happy Paper Hearts online shop (http://www.etsy.com/shop/HappyPaperHearts)
Cactus-shaped sugar cookies—All Things Exquisite online shop (www.AllThingsExquisite.com)
Old-fashioned taffy—www.CrackerBarrel.com
Corncob fondant cupcake toppers—Parkers Flour Patch online shop (www.etsy.com/shop/parkersflourpatch)
American Indian head fondant cookie toppers—Cookie Covers online shop (www.CookieCovers.net)

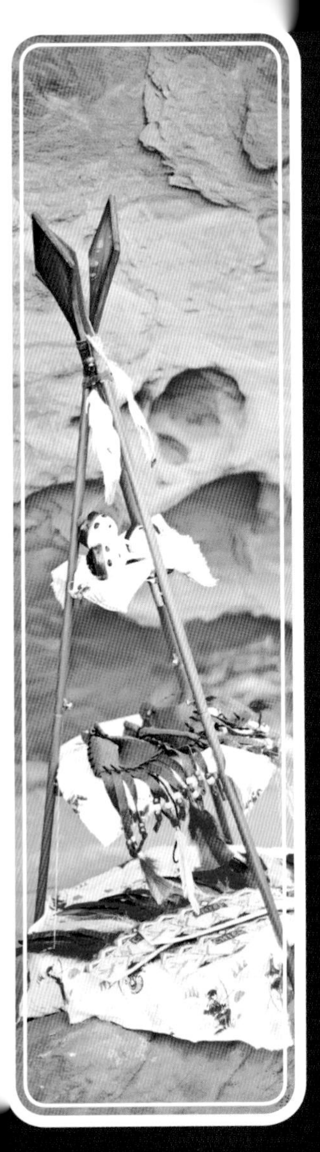

strawberry rolls
raspberry mousse
chocolate cupcakes

ELEPHANT BABY SHOWER

Photography by Lyndsey Fagerlund

www.LyndseyFagerlund.com

There is nothing more endearing than a baby elephant and her mother. When planning this baby shower to celebrate the birth of an upcoming baby girl, I wanted to capture that sweet love shared between a mother and her baby.

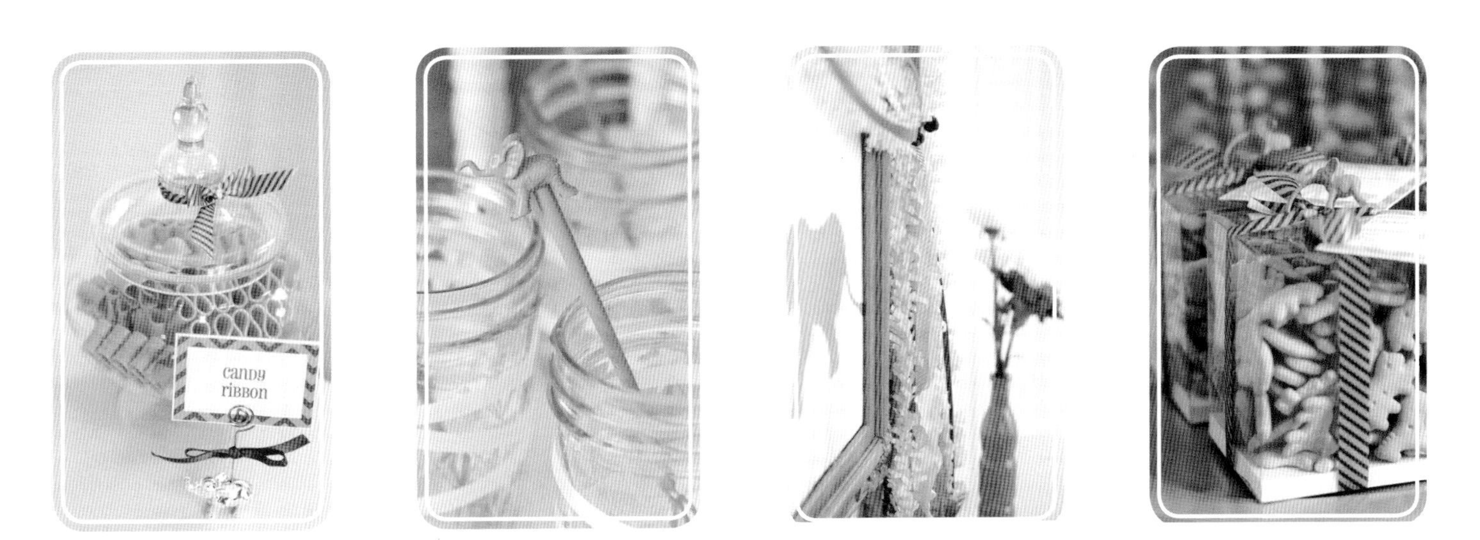

PINK WAS OBVIOUSLY the main color scheme. From cake stands to ribbon and vases to plates, pink definitely set the tone for the event.

AS A BACKDROP, I used a vinyl elephant decal in a large painted frame as the focal point. It was accented with fanned tissue flowers and various ribbons in all shapes, colors, and textures. They were hung to form a small curtain-like design. The pink tablecloth was accented with a long strand of pink pom trimming, scalloped in a fun pattern. Small silver elephant place card holders, accented with a delicate pink bow, were used to display food labels. Old fashioned pink ribbon candy was placed in a large apothecary jar. A cute, striped bow adorned the lid. Rather than filling tall apothecary jars with the usual candy and trinkets, I lined them with beautiful pink-toned flowers and wrapped the jars in pretty striped ribbon.

I PLACED A PRETTY RUFFLE CAKE at the center of the main table. It was topped with a strand of pink elephant cut outs, sewn together in a parade and tied between two elephant swizzle sticks. I attached another strand of the pink pom trimming to the edge of the cake stand.

I USED VARIOUS BABY FURNITURE to display different party elements. A wooden high chair was painted pink to hold the party favor boxes, and a matching wooden changing table was used as the drink station.

WHO SAYS THAT YOU CAN'T PAINT PEANUTS? With a needle and thread, I strung hundreds of peanuts for a fun and unique party backdrop. Once the peanuts were all threaded into several strands, I painted them pink, using canned aerosol spray.

FOR THE FAVORS, I filled clear plastic boxes from my shop with animal crackers. They were accented with striped ribbon and small pink elephant figurines. Attached was a note that read, "Animal Crackers Just for You . . . Elephants & Friends from the Zoo."

SMALL CANNING JARS were used as drinking glasses, and like the other party elements, were accented with pink ribbon. Elephant swizzle sticks were placed in each glass. On the drink menu—Italian sodas. Soda water was placed in a large apothecary beverage dispenser. Guests were able to choose from several specialty syrups for flavoring.

animal crackers just for you...
Elephants & Friends from the zoo!
Thanks for coming!
Love

PLASTIC CHINESE SOUP SPOONS were used to hold cheesecake bites. To make these, simply line the bottom of the spoons with graham cracker crust. Then place the prepared cheesecake filling in a ziplock bag. Make a small cut in one corner of the bag and carefully squeeze the cheesecake out through the hole onto each spoon. To finish, top each cheesecake with a dab of strawberry sauce.

PAINTED METAL TUBS were turned upside down to look like elephant steps. Darling cupcakes with fondant elephant toppers from TwoSugarBabies.com were placed on each elephant step.

RASPBERRY MOUSSE was layered in small clear cups to create delicious mini parfaits (recipe on facing page).

~Make Your Own~

Rasberry Mousse

{Makes 12 servings}

2 12-ounce packages frozen raspberries, thawed
1 14-ounce can sweetened condensed milk
1 Tablespoon plus 2 teaspoons cornstarch
2 Tablespoons orange juice
2 cups heavy whipping cream, whipped

In a saucepan, combine raspberries and cornstarch until blended. Bring to a boil; stir and cook for 2½ minutes, or until thickened. Transfer the mixture to a large bowl to refrigerate until chilled. Set aside half of the raspberry mixture. To the remaining half, add condensed milk and orange juice; stir until well blended. Fold in whipped cream. Spoon ¼ cup cream mixture into each of the 12 parfait dishes or glasses. Layer each glass with ¼ cup reserved raspberry mixture and another ¼ cup cream mixture. Refrigerate until serving.

Do you want to re-create this party?

Combined with the templates on the CD and the party details in this chapter, the list below will give you everything you need to get started!

Paper honeycomb flowers, fanned tissue flowers, paper streamers, clear favor boxes, cake stands, ribbon candy, Chinese soup spoons, clear mousse cups, ribbon, glass apothecary jars—available from Kara's Party Shop (www.KarasPartyIdeas.com/shop)
Fondant elephant cupcake toppers—Two Sugar Babies (www.twoSugarBabies.com)
Elephant Cupcake Toppers—Included on CD

ICE CREAM SOCIAL

Photography by Lyndsey Fagerlund

www. LyndseyFagerlund.com

Gather children and neighbors together and host a fun Ice Cream Social! Have everyone bring their favorite ice cream toppings while you provide the ice cream and activities. An ice cream party will be a memorable event that will bring everyone together and send them all home with a smile.

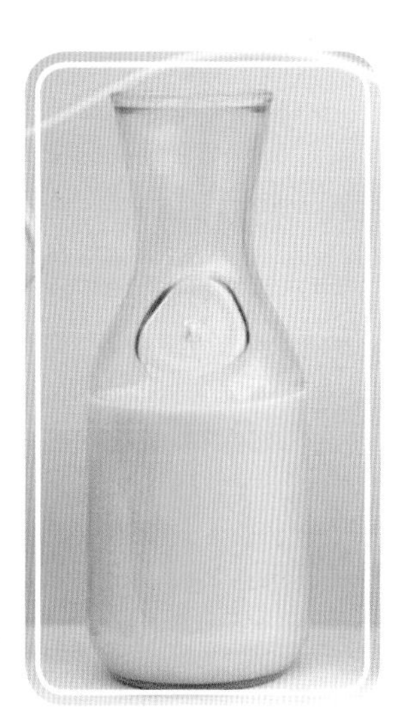

THIS IS A FAVORITE OF ALL THE PARTIES that I have designed or styled, mostly because of the rather large and unusual backdrop—a real vintage ice cream truck! Found among online classifieds, the 1965 Ford was old and rusty and needed a lot of TLC. The project was one I was excited to take on, though. I love transforming things, especially when it means refinishing something that has gone many years unnoticed. After a good scrubbing, cleaning, sanding, taping, and—finally—painting, the truck slowly started to look like new again, maybe just as it looked when it really was new, over forty years ago. It was the perfect backdrop for the best ice cream party on the block.

CONTINUING WITH THE VINTAGE FEEL, the party display included antique signs, tall retro ice cream cone money banks, old-style cake stands, and even a vintage cash register.

WHO SAYS THAT ICE CREAM has to be the only dessert at an ice cream party? Yes, it is definitely the main element, but why not add some other delectable treats and pastries to the main table?

I FOUND AN OLD ROUND TABLE at a thrift store and painted it pink to match the aqua-and-pink color scheme. The light blue and white striped table cover was actually wrapping paper, secured underneath the table with tape.

SINCE ICE CREAM is better with a cherry on top, I incorporated cherries into the party theme, as well.

SMALL CHERRY PIES were placed on a pink cake stand atop the dessert table. Also on the table was a cute little step stool, which I painted blue and used as a shelf to hold the ice cream cone–themed sugar cookies and cupcakes. The cupcakes were adorned with upside down mini ice cream cones and melted chocolate (creating the look of melting ice cream). Pink coconut marshmallow treats were placed in a cute, scalloped yellow tray and were topped with coordinating paper ice cream tags, which are included on the CD. Sugar cones filled with cotton candy were placed in a cup shaped like an ice cream cone.

strawberry
Ice
chocolate
ICE CREAM CUPS & SPOONS

CHERRY
CHERRY

Ice Cream
5¢

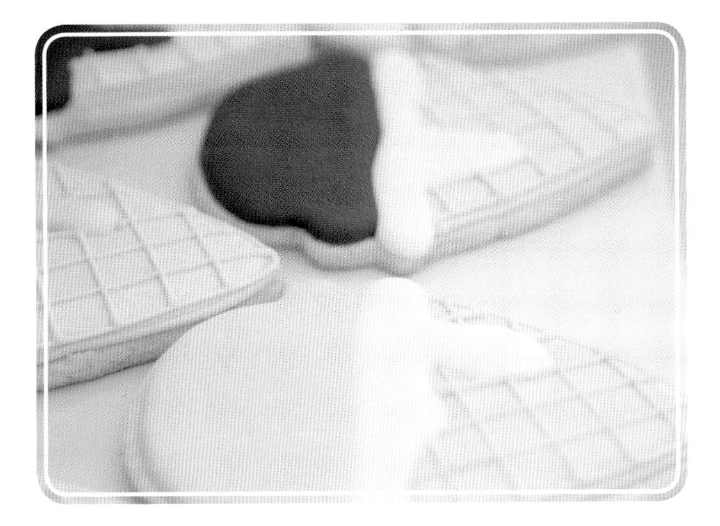

EASILY DRESS UP a store-bought cake with ice cream cones! Evenly space the cones a few inches apart around the outer edge of the cake. Then create the look of ice cream using piped frosting and cherries. A super-easy and adorable ice cream cake!

WAFER CONES WERE LINED with wrapping paper and filled with pink malt balls. Chocolate covered cake pops were placed in sugar cones, creating an ice cream treat that wouldn't melt away.

~ Make Your Own ~

Homemade Ice Cream

1 pint half & half

⅓ cup sugar

¼ cup instant pudding mix

10 cups ice

1½ cups rock salt

- Combine all ingredients except ice and salt in a small, one-pound can or a quart-size plastic freezer bag.
- To make the ice cream using cans, place the one-pound can (duct tape the lid closed) inside a larger three-pound can and surround the smaller can with ice and salt. Duck tape the lid on and invite the kids to kick the can around for about 15 minutes.
- To make it in a bag, put the sealed quart-size plastic bag inside a gallon bag. Surround the small bag with ice and salt and tightly close the larger bag. Invite the kids to shake the bag for 10–15 minutes.

Do you want to re-create this party?

Combined with the templates on the CD and the party details in this chapter, the list below will give you everything you need to get started!

Candy, push pop containers, milk bottles, brown swirl treat bags, cardboard cherry baskets—Kara's Party Shop (www.KarasPartyIdeas.com/Shop)
Party printables (Invite, signs, tags, cupcake toppers)—Included on CD (designed by www.PaperAndPigtailsParty.com)
Ice Cream Cone sugar cookies—Stephanie J's Creations (www.Etsy.com/Shop/StephanieJsCreations)
Fondant cherry cookie toppers—Mommy Cr8s (www.Etsy.com/Shop/Mommycr8s)
Ice cream vinyl decal—Tweet Heart Wall Art (www.TweetHeartWallArt.com)

WELCOME TO THE CARNIVAL
RESTROOMS
BIRTHDAY
GAMES
PRIZES
Food & Drinks
PARTY
CELEBRA

CIRCUS TRAIN BIRTHDAY PARTY

Photography by Valerie Hart Photography

www.ValerieHartPhotography.com

Come one, come all, and join the fun! Sean and Emily's Three-Ring Birthday Circus Train has arrived! Complete with clowns, tickets, popcorn, hot dogs, candy, games, prizes, cupcakes, and even a carousel, there is definitely no end to the entertainment at this party!

THE MOMENT I FOUND a lovely carousel outside of City Hall in St. George, Utah, my mind just couldn't stop dreaming of all the fun things this Circus Train Birthday Party could include. I set the stage with three circus train cars, which I made out of baby cribs. I transformed the regular white cribs into a real life circus train by adding painted wooden scroll pieces and paper bunting for decoration and fanned flowers to serve as wheels. I then connected the train cars using red and blue crepe paper. Each train car provided the perfect space to display much of the party food, treats, and decor. To get started, I lined each car with red and white wrapping paper.

THE FOCAL POINT of the first circus train car was the darling Balancing Elephant Cake made by Marcee Kitchen of Dippidee. The other fun circus items surrounding the cake included toy animals that I "dressed up" with paint and ribbon; a miniature metal Ferris Wheel dispenser with bowls full of toys and treats; a sweet vintage Humpty Dumpty Lumps penny candy tin; a rotating wooden container filled with colored paper straws, candy mustaches, bright party blow outs, and candy peanuts; strongman dumbbells made with striped straws and round suckers; animal crackers; and more!

THE MIDDLE CIRCUS TRAIN CAR held a large faux cake that I made out of hat boxes and tickets. Next to the cake were cute three-ring circus train boxes and ceramic circus letters. I placed fun cups shaped like circus tents at the front of the table, and next to them, put a darling cupcake tower made with a kit from my shop. The cupcake tower was accented with fun silver cording, yellow pom ribbon, blue crepe paper, and a cute mini bunting banner (banner template included on the CD). It was finished with a clown nose at the top! The circus clown cupcakes couldn't have been cuter sitting there amongst ceramic circus figurines. The circus tent–shaped sugar cookies, ordered from AllThingsExquisite.com were a hit, as were the "peanut" cups filled with orange candy circus peanuts. Peeking out from the back of the train car was a darling vintage "Tiddlywinks" clown game and a "Circus Parade" book.

CIRCUS
PARADE
PHYLLIS R. FENNER
Illustrated by Lee Ames

COME ONE,
COME ALL!
BIG TOP
FOR: Sean's 5th Birthday
DATE: Saturday, February 18th
TIME: 3:00 pm
PLACE: St George City Carousel
RSVP:

STRONGMAN
DUMBBELLS

THE THIRD CIRCUS TRAIN CAR held the majority of the food. I love the miniature electric hot dog warmer that I used to heat the hot dogs. On the opposite side of the table, I also had a matching popcorn machine full of the delicious buttery stuff. In the center of the train car was a white metal tub with rubber duckies inside.There were also several sizes of apothecary jars that I filled with suckers, miniature rainbow candies, and red gumballs.

I ORDERED the splendid clown cake pops from the online Etsy shop of Autumn Lynn's Chocolate Sin's. They couldn't have been cuter in the stacked silver milk bottles! I made "lion tamer whips" out of chocolate licorice and placed them in a clear shallow glass bowl. I also filled cute carnival treat boxes with cupcakes for the guests, just in case they didn't get enough sweets!

PAPER TICKETS are so versatile and cute that I couldn't resist using them a lot throughout this party! The first train car featured vintage suitcases covered in white tickets. The focal point of the middle train car was the ticket "cake" I made, mentioned earlier. On the food train car, I used tickets as napkin rings to secure forks to red and yellow polka-dot napkins. I also wrapped tickets around the ketchup and mustard bottles.

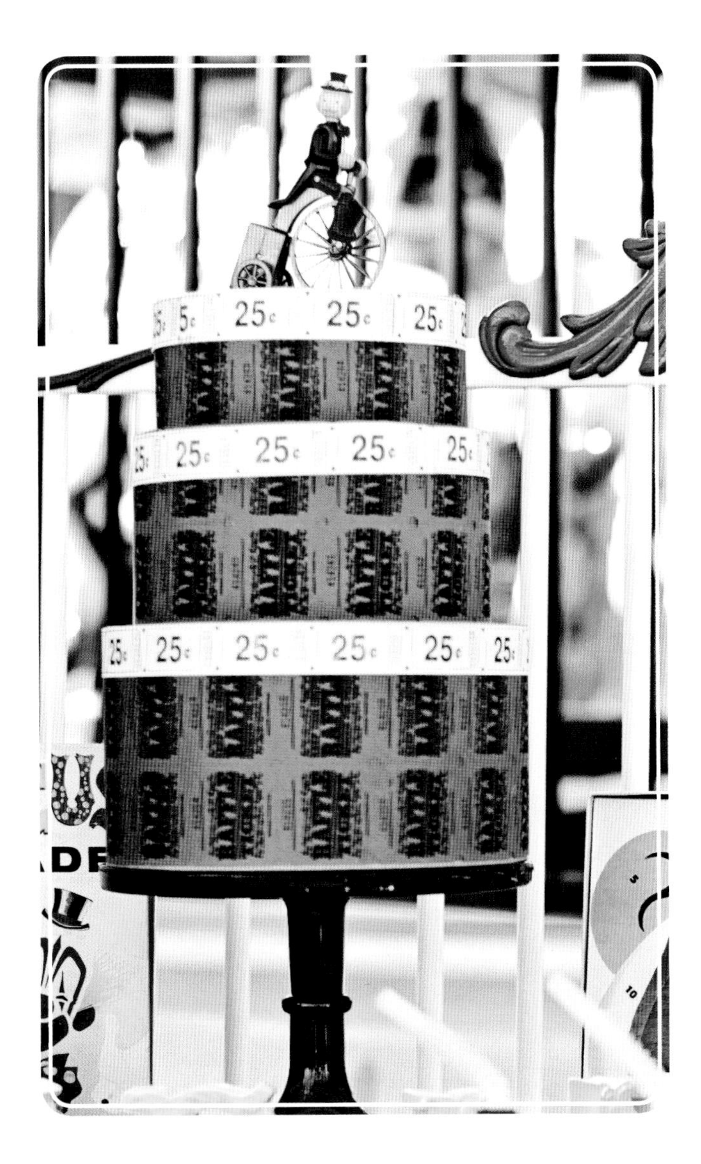

AS GUESTS ARRIVED AT THE PARTY, they were greeted with a happy ceramic clown on top of stacked ticket rolls. I made a fun wreath out of clown noses and tickets to place on the table next to the clown. Guests also walked past a bright ticket booth. I made the booth with a wooden puppet stand, painted and decorated to match the circus theme and colors. To add to the ambiance, I strung a red, white, and yellow felt "celebrate" banner between the ticket booth and the "Welcome to the Carnival" sign.

LION
TAMER
WHIPS
Movie Time
Popcorn

RAFFLE
TICKET

25¢
TICKET
POPCORN

KEEP THIS COUPON
RAFFLE
REDEEM FOR PRIZES

THREE-RING
CIRCUS
COMING TO YOUR TOWN!

TIME FOR A TREAT!

PEANUT
PEANUT

25¢
Pop
Shoppe
RAFFLE
TICKET
TICKET

HOT DOG
Hot Dogs

PRIZE

The Pop Shoppe
RING
TOSS

ALL OF THE PARTY GUESTS had a chance to have their picture taken at a festive carnival-themed photo booth! I made the booth using PVC pipe, hot glue, and colorful polka-dot fabric. I strung a homemade, fabric "Happy Birthday" banner across the back of the booth. To the side of the booth was a gumball machine and balloons tied to a yellow ducky balloon weight. I found a vintage suitcase online and filled it with photo booth props like silly glasses, hats, noses, bow ties, gloves, a xylophone, and even a rubber chicken! I think that it looked just like a traveling circus clown's suitcase would.

THE GUESTS ALSO played the famous carnival game "Ring Toss" using rope rings and some old "Pop Shop" glass bottles that I found at an antique shop.

AS THE CHILDREN moved through the various party activities, they collected tickets. Once they had enough tickets they were able to pick a prize off the prize wall. I made the prize wall using a wooden free-standing chalkboard that I covered in fabric and topped with a "prizes" sign. To make the prizes, I filled clear cellophane bags with plastic balls, games, noise makers, and yo-yos. The bags were then sealed with striped wrapping paper and blue crepe paper streamers and secured to the wall with clothes pins.

WELCOME TO THE CARNIVAL
RESTROOMS
ATTRACTIONS

CIRCUS

PHOTO
BOOTH

Enjoy Coca-Cola

RAFFLE
KEEP THIS COUPON
CARNIVAL
BARKER'S
BREW
BIG
BIG
STRONG
MAN
SUPER SODA
CLOWN
FIZZIE DRINK
SUPER-FIZZIE, EXTRA-BUBBLY,
INCREDIBLY-WACKY
SILLY DRINK!
CIDER

Coca-Cola

I ARRANGED MASON-JAR GLASSES on a small round table. Behind the glasses was a fun lollipop display. I made the display using an old Coca-Cola® crate, some Styrofoam, and various fun and colorful lollipops and jawbreaker pops. I strung a delicate bunting flag banner (made with tickets and silver pipe cleaner) between two glittery batons nestled in the back of the crate. There were also two glass apothecary jars on the table, filled with yummy cookies.

A DRINK STATION was situated in an old galvanized bucket. I used two long wooden dowels to hang the "Drinks" banner I made using an ornate circus font for the lettering. Inside the bucket were old fashioned–style soda bottles. There were also water bottles labeled "Circus Water" (label template included on the CD).

Do you want to re-create this party?

Combined with the templates on the CD and the party details in this chapter, the list below will give you everything you need to get started!

Directional carnival sign, "Celebrate" fabric banner, striped fanned flowers (wheels), tickets, circus tent cupcake stand, circus tent–shaped cups, silver milk bottles, polka-dot napkins, apothecary jars, lollipops, ketchup/mustard containers, rubber duckies, popcorn bags, circus drink labels, hot dog containers, tissue bunting flags, clown noses, jumbo bow ties, clown gloves, clown hats, rubber chicken, candy sticks, party blow outs, paper straws, carnival gable boxes, cake stands, marshmallow peanuts, red-and-white striped wrapping paper, plastic clown cupcake toppers, embellished paper clown toppers, candles, toy prizes, crepe paper, candy mustaches, suckers, duckie balloon weights, gumballs, balloons, crepe paper, Big Top cupcake/treat boxes, clown costumes, striped cupcake liners—Available from Kara's Party Shop (www.KarasPartyIdeas.com/Shop)

Invitations, tags, labels, water bottle wrappers—Included on CD

Circus Tent sugar cookies—All Things Exquisite (www.AllThingsExquisite.com)

Cake and cupcakes—Marcee Kitchen of Dippidee (www.Dippidee.com)

Clown cake pops—Autumn Lynn's Chocolate Sins online shop (http://www.etsy.com/shop/AutumnLynnsSins)

Birthday notes for Jane
Happy Birthday
Emma Jane's Dress Shoppe
TOM THUMB

VINTAGE DICK AND JANE BIRTHDAY PARTY

Photography by Valerie Hart Photography

www.ValerieHartPhotography.com

See *Spot run! Run, Spot, run!* Do you remember the classic Dick and Jane books that helped children learn how to read in the 1940s and '50s? This precious second birthday party for a little girl named Jane is full of vintage items and sweet Dick and Jane memorabilia. Seeing this party will take you back to the era in which these books and darling characters thrived.

WHAT MORE FITTING THEME could Jane have had for her second birthday party than vintage Dick and Jane? One glance at any element of this party will remind you of a simpler time when typewriters, red tricycles, and milk glass abounded. Personally, I absolutely love anything vintage right now, so the moment I found out the party theme, I literally went through my home collecting vintage items to incorporate into the party design. I decided to set up the display tables on the back porch of an older home, enhancing the reminiscent feel of the party. I love how it all turned out!

MY PARTY DISPLAY BEGAN with a cream bookshelf, which I refinished and painted a couple of years ago. In my search for vintage items, I came across some fun board letters with replica Dick and Jane images on them. I used the board letters to spell out the birthday girl's name on the top shelf of the bookcase. In front of the letter 'A' was a darling, vintage-inspired pink toy bike. I put a white milk-glass vase filled with roses next to the bike. On the second shelf was an adorable antique cake carrier, which I found on Etsy. Old, clear glass trays were carefully stacked next to the cake carrier. A banner, made with scrapbook paper and ribbon, was strung across the front of the second shelf. When I came across the vintage-themed scrapbook paper pack at the store, I was so excited. It couldn't have matched the theme or color palette of the party more perfectly!

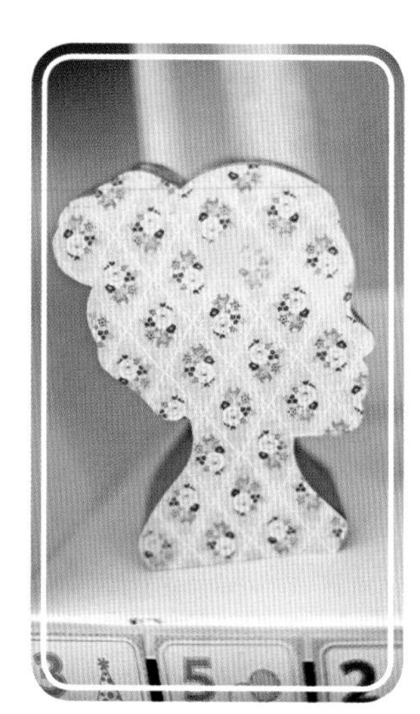

UNDERNEATH THE BANNER was an antique aqua milk-glass cake stand, holding lemon Cakebites® from The Sweet Tooth Fairy. Next to the cake stand were glass saucers that matched the clear glass trays and a stack of antique pink and blue plates.

THE NEXT SHELF DOWN held a silhouette bookend (which I covered in vintage-inspired floral paper) and another milk-glass vase, holding tulips. An Anso Shur Shot camera, purchased at an antique shop, was at the end of the shelf. For a simple and fun party activity, I filled some charming quilted jelly jars with bubble solution. I attached vintage skeleton keys to the jars using a strip of dainty floral fabric. The skeleton keys served as bubble wands!

ON THE BOTTOM SHELF of the bookcase was a small, round glass serving tray holding vintage-style yellow and white candy wafers. The backdrop to the tray was a fabulous thrift-store find, a cute antique book with a darling floral design. In the middle of the bottom shelf were "Happy Birthday" treat bags from my shop. On the right side of the shelf was a small bowl filled with mini paper treat bags.

TO CREATE A GUEST BOOK DISPLAY, I borrowed a darling old schoolhouse desk from my friend and placed a vintage Tom Thumb typewriter (purchased on Etsy) on top of it. I made a cute collage out of scrapbook paper (from the same paper pack I used for the banner) to go inside of the typewriter. Next to the typewriter, I laid another piece of scrapbook paper for guests to write sweet notes to Jane. I filled an antique blue mason jar with pink carnations and set it on the desk as well. On the seat of the desk was a fun, retro wall hanging with an additional signing page for the guests to use once the other one filled up.

WHEN I PICTURE DICK AND JANE, I see one of them pulling a red wagon. My friend had an antique wagon that matched my vision precisely, so I borrowed it to use as an additional display for the party. I pulled the wagon up near the bookshelf and set a small plate with cupcakes on top inside it. The rest of the space inside the wagon was used to hold birthday gifts as Jane's guests arrived. The wagon also served as a fun toy for the kids to play with later on.

IN THE MIDDLE OF THE PORCH was an antique Singer sewing table, with the actual sewing machine still inside. I used book pages (taken out of a replica Dick and Jane book, not an original) and dainty, light-aqua ribbon to make a banner to hang on the front of the sewing table. Atop the table was a light-green hobnail cake stand holding some cream cheese lace sugar cookies from Dippidee. My favorite element of the sewing table display was the darling vintage children's books, which were stacked on top of each other to provide a base for another hobnail cake stand. I placed some lemon cupcakes inside various patterned cupcake liners and arranged them on the cake stand. I made cupcake toppers by punching out images from a digital online download with a craft punch and gluing them to sucker sticks. Next to the stack of books were two vintage vases filled with roses, baby's breath, and pink carnations. There was also a small blue-and-tan ice cream box overflowing with white daisies. I found a metal bike wall hanging at a local home store and painted it blue to match the party colors. I used it to prop up some more Dick and Jane board letters, spelling out "TWO" since it was Jane's second birthday.

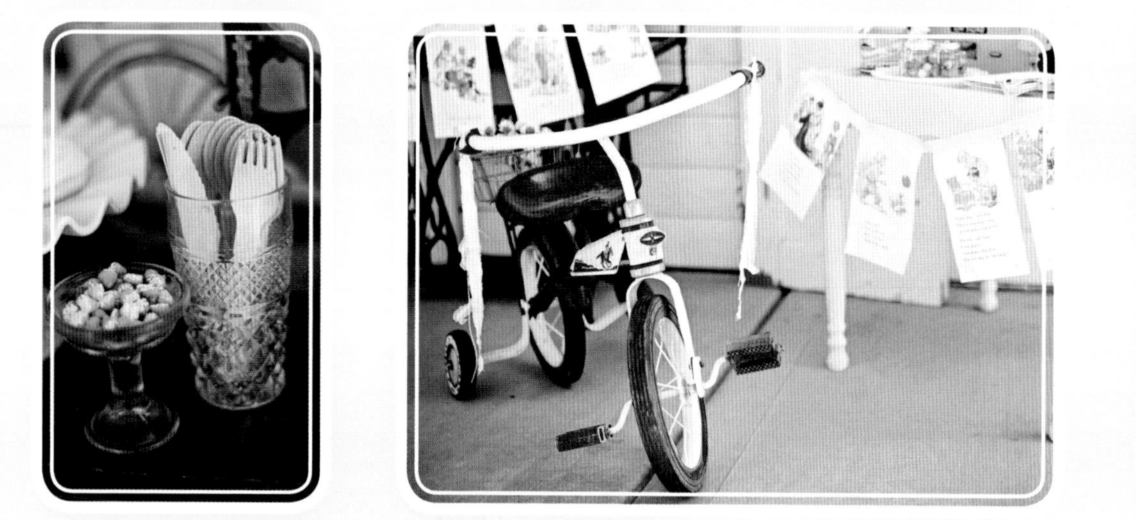

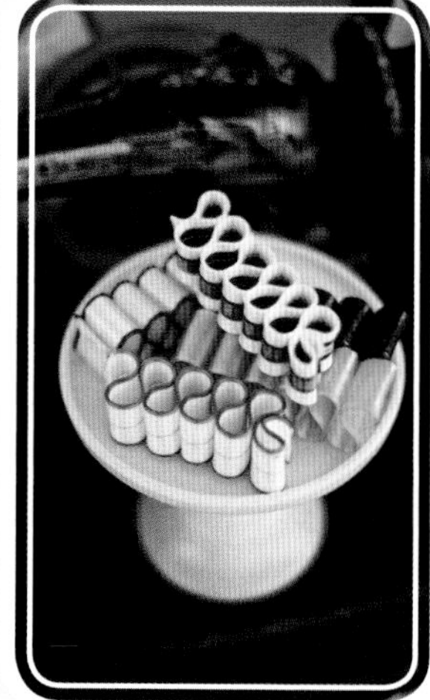

Look, Sally.
I see something.
I see Baby Sally.
Little Baby Sally.
Look, look.
See funny Baby Sally.
Run, Puff.
Run, Puff, run.
Run, run, run.
Jump, jump, jump.
"Look, Jane," said Dick.
"Here is something funny.
Can you guess what it is?"
"Oh, yes," said Jane.
"I can guess.
I can guess what it is.
This will help me find Sally."
Oh, oh, oh.
Spot can find Dick.
Spot can find Jane.
Oh, oh.
Spot can help Sally.
Spot can play.

ONE PINT
CREAM CO.
NEW MEXICO

I PLACED WOODEN UTENSILS in a vintage tumbler and set a small, pink glass candy dish—filled with miniature button candies—in front of the utensils. On a pink milk-glass cake stand was beautiful colored ribbon candy, a definite old-time favorite! I filled a frame with more cute matching paper and placed the frame, along with a vintage doll found at an antique shop, on the front edge of the sewing table. Behind the frame on another pink milk-glass cake stand was the adorable birthday cake (which was made by Marcee Kitchen of Dippidee).

I WISH I COULD SAY that the precious vintage red bike was mine, but it's not. It was also borrowed from a friend to use at the party. Jane and her friends had so much fun riding down the sidewalk on it (and pulling along the red wagon, too). It couldn't have been cuter. I loved the idea of placing delicate yellow flowers in the basket of the bike. What a sweet touch!

THE FINAL PARTY DISPLAY was on a small, pink, wooden table. I strung a second Dick and Jane book-page banner across the front of the table. For party favors, I filled small glass jars with marbles, secured their screw-top lids and tied baker's twine around the tops. The jars were displayed on a white milk-glass plate.

TOM THUMB

ROCK CANDY STICKS were placed upside down in an old crystal tumbler. A pink Therm-A-Jug, another antique-shop find, was filled with strawberry lemonade and pink and blue paper straws were put in a small milk-glass creamer pitcher. I also filled another antique ice cream container, this time pink, with white daisies and placed it on the front corner of the table. Striped paper plates and cute bicycle napkins sat on the other corner of the table.

DELICIOUS ICED SHORTBREAD COOKIES from Dippidee were arranged on an antique pink glass pastry plate near the back of the display. An antique door was leaned against the wall next to the pink table for extra depth and to add to the vintage feel.

I STRUNG TOGETHER vintage replica handkerchiefs from my shop to make a graceful banner, which I hung above the party tables. It definitely added the finishing touch to the soiree.

Do you want to re-create this party?

Combined with the templates on the CD and party details in this chapter, the list below will give you everything you need to get started!

Cupcake liners, rock candy sticks, sucker sticks, ribbon, baker's twine, screw-top marble jars, handkerchiefs, small glass milk bottles, ribbon candy, Sixlets®, apothecary jars, paper straws, wooden utensils, candy, paper straws, striped paper plates, marbles, cake stands, paper punch (to make cupcake toppers)—Kara's Party Shop (www.KarasPartyIdeas.com/Shop)

Iced shortbread cookies, cream cheese lace sugar cookies, cake—Marcee Kitchen of Dippidee (www.Dippidee.com)

Lemon Cakebites®—The Sweet Tooth Fairy (www.thesweettoothfairy.com)

Scrapbook paper pack—Jo-Ann Fabric & Craft

G
K
I
DANGER

SUPERHERO BIRTHDAY PARTY

Photography by Lyndsey Fagerlund

www.LyndseyFagerlund.com

B*am! Boom! Pow! Zap!* Get your superhero capes on for this action. What better way to celebrate a child's birthday than with a superhero party? Nothing says "I think you're extraordinary" more than a celebration revolving around characters who are just that!

I DESIGNED THIS PARTY for my two little boys and their friends. I wanted the party to be bold and fun, creating a mini superhero world for all the guests.

I ALWAYS THINK THAT THE INVITATION sets the tone for a party. I wanted my superhero invitation to be fun and different, and I came up with the perfect way! Step one involved dressing my birthday boys in their superman capes and taking them to a nearby black asphalt parking lot. (Make sure it's an empty parking lot! We went to a church parking lot during the week so there were no cars). Next, I used white chalk and drew swish lines and a cityscape onto the asphalt.

TO CREATE THE FRONT OF THE INVITE, I had my older son lie on the asphalt above the buildings (as though he was flying over them) while I snapped a photo. For the back of the invite, I drew a large earth and more swish lines. I then took a photo of my younger son lying on the asphalt between the world and the swish lines. He looked like Superman lifting the world with his mighty strength. At home, I added text and the party details in a photo editing program and printed the invitations double-sided.

AN EASY BALLOON WREATH hanging on the front door was made with a Styrofoam wreath form, un-inflated balloons, and pushpins.

WHEN THE PARTY KICKED OFF, all of the guests received a superhero muscle shirt upon arrival. Then, as they waited for everyone to arrive, they colored a giant superhero backdrop that was laid out on our cement patio.

CAPTAIN AMERICA PEZ DISPENSERS, party blow outs, plastic superhero rings, and other favors for the guests were placed in various glass jars and trays throughout the three display tables.

I
DANGER

I
DANGER

HAPPY BIRTHDAY
KADEN & GAVIN!

During the party, the children had their faces painted to look like their favorite superhero, used their super powers to lift a heavy barbell, and stood behind a car-raising photo op.

The guests also "sprayed the evil villain" (with silly string), colored superhero activity books, and flew away with lightning wings on their shoes!

I prepared lightning bolts cut out of yellow card stock that we attached to children's shoelaces. You can make your own using the lightning bolt template found on the included CD.

I decided to create three display tables, each in the theme of a different superhero. I decorated the main table in a fun Superman theme. The large, customized cityscape hanging behind it really added to the ambiance. The focal point, though, was the fabulous three-tiered cake made by Jennifer Hanna of Sweeten Your Day Cakes. It was a representation of the three superheroes that were featured at each table—Batman, Superman, and Captain America. Wonder Woman "lassos" (licorice), telephone booth–shaped cookies, and Super Ropes were also set out on the table. Another fun element of the Superman table was the "Clark Kent Disguise Station." It was set up on top of a large briefcase, complete with superman eyeglasses and paper business ties. "Daily Planet" yo-yos were also part of the display. The children had fun dressing up in the items and posing for pictures in front of a red phone booth backdrop.

WONDER WOMAN
LASSO'S!

SPRAY THE
VILLAIN!

DAILY PLANTET
YOYO'S!

TELEPHONE

"SUPER" ROPES!

THE BATMAN-THEMED table featured an assortment of sweets. Across the front of the table, I strung a banner made out of cardboard 3-D glasses. Below that was a second banner made out of superhero cards and blue ribbon. Among the favorite treats were "Pow!" and "Bam!" sugar cookies (ordered online from www.Batches.Etsy.com), cupcake pops (made using plastic push pop containers from my shop and mini cupcakes), and barbells (made using round cherry suckers and red straws).

OTHER FUN TREATS were cupcakes with edible fondant toppers (ordered online from EdibleDetails.com), ring pops, Astro Pop popsicles, skyscraper cookies, and pop rocks. I also created superhero pops using suckers, tissue paper, and tiny printable capes and eye masks. The fun cape and mask templates are included on the CD.

HERO MEDALS!

POWER DIP!

CORN "POPS"!

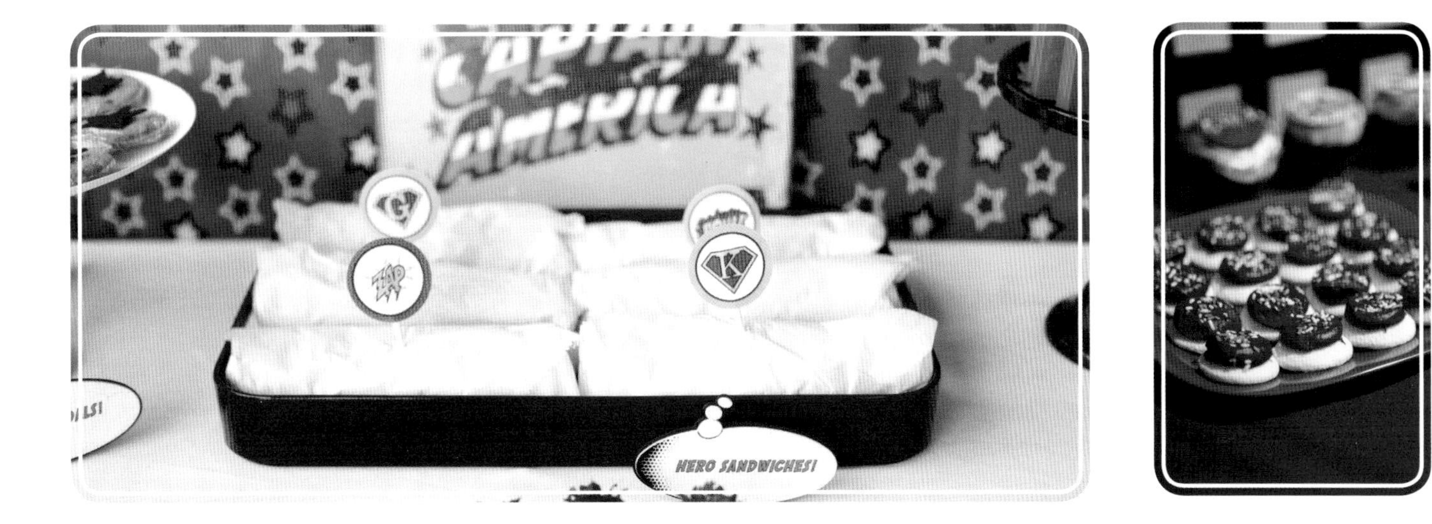

THE MAJORITY OF THE SUPER FOOD was on the Captain America table. There were lightning rod watermelon pieces, hero sandwiches, superhero strawberries (made with white Wilton Candy Melts® and blue sprinkles), Corn Pops, hero cookie medals (made with chocolate chip cookies wrapped in cellophane and attached to ribbon), and veggies with power dip. To make the veggies and dip, I put a spoonful of ranch dressing (aka "power dip") in the bottom of white nut cups and then added lightning rod–shaped yellow pepper strips, along with carrots and snap peas. It was a fun, healthy snack for the kids to eat, and just the right size too!

AFTER EATING, the children had a blast as they were surrounded by a super bubble. Each child stood on a stool in the middle of a small pool filled with a homemade bubble solution (instructions found on facing page). A hula-hoop was quickly lifted out of the pool and above the child's head to create the ginormous cylindrical bubble. Our photographer snapped pictures of each child as they were inside the bubble for them to take home.

~ Make Your Own ~

HOMEMADE BUBBLE SOLUTION

19 L (5 gallons) distilled water

2.5 L (10 cups) Dawn® dish soap (non-antibacterial)

1.2 L (5 cups) Glycerin (optional)

Children's hard plastic swimming pool

Hula Hoop

- **Set the pool in an area that is away from any wind. Mix distilled water with Dawn® Dish Soap in the swimming pool.**
- **To create stronger bubbles, add Glycerin to the mix. The bubble solution will get better with time, so if possible, allow your mixture to sit overnight.**
- **When you're ready to start the activity, place the hula-hoop at the bottom of the pool. If desired, put a small stool in the center of the swimming pool so children won't have to remove their shoes.**
- **Have a child get in the pool (or on the stool), and quickly and steadily lift the hula-hoop straight out of the water over the child's head.**

Hint: *If your bubble isn't forming it is probably because you are lifting the hula-hoop too slowly.*

Do you want to re-create this party?

Combined with the templates on the CD and the party details in this chapter, the list below will give you everything you need to get started!

Push pop containers, balloons, jars, ring pops, super rope, white nut cups, Wilton Candy Melts®, Superman rings, party blow outs, Captain America Pez dispensers, straws, Strong Man photo op backdrop, Superman glasses, sparkler candles, mini suitcases, tissue paper, yo-yos, 3-D glasses for banner, Captain America rings, Silly String, round suckers, Tootsie Pops, superhero favors—Kara's Party Shop (www.KarasPartyIdeas.com/Shop)

Sucker Hero and Super Pop printable capes and masks, drink masks—Included on CD (created by www.PaperAndPigtailsParty.com)

Face painting—Denise Cold of Painted Party Face Painting, Orem, UT (www.PaintedParty.com)

Cake—Jennifer Hanna (www.Etsy.com/Shop/SweetenYourDay)

Cityscape backdrop, square lollipop covers, circle tags, cupcake toppers—Anders Ruff Custom Designs (http://www.AndersRuff.com)

Fondant cupcake toppers—Edible Details (www.EdibleDetails.com)

Comic Strip and Sky Scraper sugar cookies—Batches (www.Batches.Etsy.com)

Coca-Cola
Coca-Cola
Coca-Cola

SOCK HOP BIRTHDAY PARTY

Photography by Valerie Hart Photography

www.ValerieHartPhotography.com

Come on, baby, let's rock 'n' roll! This Sock Hop birthday party will make you want to twist and shout. The party was set in a 1950s-inspired diner, complete with diner-style food, fabulous '50s desserts, old-fashioned drinks, '50s clothes, and more. Get ready to have your saddle shoes knocked right off!

I'VE WANTED TO STYLE a Sock Hop party for a long time now and finally got the chance! The party was held at Iceberg Drive Inn, where two families decided to come together to celebrate their children's combined birthdays. The diner setting couldn't have been better for the occasion. The booths, the high bar complete with stools, the black-and-red color palette—everything was perfect.

THE PARTY had a lot of creative elements, starting with the invitations (template is included on the CD). For a unique and memorable twist, the invitations were delivered along with old records I found at a thrift store. The fun invites definitely set the tone for the occasion.

THE TWO BIRTHDAY CHILDREN, Brigham and Kaitlyn, were dressed from head to toe in darling Sock Hop attire. Kaitlyn was dressed in a yellow poodle skirt and a white button-up blouse, accented with a cute black scarf. To top off her outfit, she wore adorable poodle socks (ordered from an online Etsy shop) and, of course, black-and-white saddle shoes! A black-and-white checked ribbon and a ribbon decorated with cherries were both tied in her high ponytail. Brigham looked like James Dean himself in his sharp, striped muscle shirt with rolled sleeves. Even his hair resembled the handsome '50s movie star. A black leather jacket, jeans, and Converse™ hi-tops completed Brigham's retro look.

IN A CORNER BOOTH, I set up a small party display showcasing fun '50s inspired desserts, food, and favors. I made a dessert stand by gluing a metal rod between two records (thrift stores always have a ton of records). The top tier of the stand held an assortment of darling sock hop–themed cookies—jukeboxes, saddle shoes, sunglasses, and poodle skirts—that I ordered from www.AllThingsExquisite.com. Displayed on the bottom tier were super-cute hamburger cupcakes made by Jennifer Hanna of Sweeten Your Day Cakes. A plate printed with an image of a vintage soda fountain held miniature pies (made by Dippidee) topped with fondant cherries ordered online from the Etsy shop Mommy Cr8s.

THREE SMALL, CLEAR GLASS JARS were each filled with candy—one with yellow rock candy, one with red gumballs, and the third with brown root beer candies. The jars were all tipped on their sides, just like they would be in an old-fashioned soda shoppe. I filled several glass ice cream sundae dishes with yummy vanilla cupcakes piled high with vanilla frosting and topped with cherries. The cupcakes, made by The Sweet Tooth Fairy, were the perfect way to have the look of retro ice cream sundaes without having to worry about anything melting. For drinks, old-fashioned Coca-Cola® bottles were paired with red-and-white striped paper straws, attached with red baker's twine.

THE AMAZING CAKE was made by Jennifer Hanna of Sweeten Your Day Cakes. I loved so many things about it, including the records, music notes, black-and-white tiles, dancing couple, and jukebox! I hung a pair of jumbo plush dice from the side of the cake stand for added flair.

TO MAKE PARTY FAVORS, I filled clear cellophane bags with both red and black paper shred and then added a few old-fashioned cherry soda bottle tops and some miniature plastic records. The main gift in the party favor bags was a pair of horn-rimmed '50s-style glasses, offered in red or black. I tied the bags closed with baker's twine and ribbon decorated with cherries, and I attached little tags made with more plastic records and black-and-white checked ribbon. The party favors were displayed in a red plastic food basket near the front of the table.

WHAT ELSE COULD the guests eat at a '50s style diner other than juicy burgers and scrumptious fries? I placed hamburgers (ordered at Iceberg) in car-shaped food boxes, while the fries were served in red plastic food baskets. The nice thing about burgers and fries is that no utensils are needed! A vintage Coca-Cola® napkin holder was set nearby, though, since a lot of napkins were used instead. Next to the napkin holder was a matching straw dispenser holding red plastic straws along with black-and-white striped paper straws. To drink, the kids each got an old-fashioned Coke and a root-beer float. It was a birthday party after all!

Do you want to re-create this party?

Combined with the templates on the CD and the party details in this chapter, the list below will give you everything you need to get started!

Location—Iceberg Drive Inn (www.IcebergDriveInn.com)
Invitation templates—Included on CD
Ribbon, baker's twine, paper straws, cellophane bags, paper shred, gumballs, glass jars, lollipops, candy, baskets, horn-rimmed glasses, paper bags—Kara's Party Shop (www.KarasPartyIdeas.com/Shop)
Sock Hop cake, hamburger cupcakes— Sweeten Your Day Cakes by Jennifer Hanna (www.Etsy.com/Shop/SweetenYourDay)
Miniature pies—Dippidee (www.Dippidee.com)
Cherry-topped vanilla cupcakes—The Sweet Tooth Fairy (www.TheSweetToothFairy.com)
'50s-inspired sugar cookies—All Things Exquisite online shop (www.AllThingsExquisite.com)
Poodle skirt and socks—Hip Hop '50s online shop (www.Etsy.com/shop/HipHop50sShop)
Car food boxes—Cute Kids Food Box online shop (www.CuteKidsFoodBox.com)
Fondant cherry pie toppers—Mommy Cr8s online shop (www.Etsy.com/Shop/Mommycr8s)

CHERRY
SODA

Coca-Cola

6
Happy Birthday Shane & Emma
WOOLY GOOD
CUPCAKES

DOWN ON THE FARM PARTY

Photography by Valerie Hart Photography

www.ValerieHartPhotography.com

Saddle up, put on your boots, grab your hat, and meet us down on the farm! What better theme could there be for a birthday party for two adorable cousins, a girl and a boy, than a fun farm hoedown?

THE MINUTE I pulled into the Staheli Family Farm in Washington, Utah, I knew the search for a perfect setting for Shane and Emma's farm party was over. From tractor hay rides and a full assortment of farm animals to duck races and children's playgrounds, the Staheli Family Farm had it all!

THE MAIN PARTY TABLE was a charming wooden picnic table that I found in the local classifieds. I set it up nestled against a large stack of hay in a location central to the activities at the farm. I adorned the front edge of the table with a triangle pennant banner made out of mismatched floral fabrics and leather cording. For a unique look, I attached each pennant to the leather cording using clothes pins! To add dimension to the table, I leaned a vintage window, adorned with a coordinating banner, against the hay bales.

THE PICNIC TABLE was decorated with so many fun farm elements. I made several fabric-covered spoons and stood them up inside a small, glass jar.

AS A PARTY FAVOR, plastic honey bear containers were dressed up with miniature bandanas, cowboy hats, and ribbon. The cowboy bears couldn't have been cuter! They were arranged inside a metal container with a honeycomb design around its perimeter.

I DECORATED a three-tiered galvanized organizer with various dollhouse accessories, such as mini flour and sugar sacks and mini farm tools. The tiny rake, shovel, and hoe were peeking out from inside a ceramic milk bottle that I placed at the top of the organizer. A framed birthday card rested against a tall red metal vase that I filled with sunflowers and wheat.

FARM FRESH
HONEY
PLEASE TAKE A BEAR

welcome to the FARM

6

APPLES

KISS ME
MARKET

THE MAIN TABLE ALSO HELD the majority of the yummy farm-themed sweets. I filled a vintage metal milk-bottle carrier with six cupcakes. The cupcakes were piled high with swirled chocolate shavings, giving the appearance of sheep's wool. For a bit of humor, only five of the cupcakes were white, while the sixth was black and topped with a tag that said, "The Black Sheep." The sign on the front of the carrier read, "Wooly Good Cupcakes" (sign and tag templates included on CD). The fantastic barn cake was made by Marcee Kitchen of Dippidee. The fondant rooster weather vane was one of my favorite details of the cake. Near the cake, there was a small metal pick-up truck with miniature hay bales in its bed, which provided the perfect anchor for the darling Farm Animal Cake Pops that I ordered from the online Etsy shop of Autumn Lynn's Chocolate Sins.

OLD-FASHIONED ROOT BEER BARREL candies were put in a small galvanized watering can at the front of the table. Next to the watering can were small cherry pies piled on a farm-style plate. To add height to the table, I turned a shallow wooden bucket upside down and topped it with a small red stool. In the space between the stool and the bucket was an assortment of miniature buckets filled with candy carrots. Sitting on the stool was a fabric-lined chicken-wire basket filled with two rows of chocolate peanut butter eggs. Two miniature metal wheelbarrows filled with tiny corn on the cob candies were in front of the basket.

WILDFLOWER
SEEDS

FRESH
LEMONADE

MINI
CINNAMON
ROLLS

Gilliam
Old Fashioned
Sanded Drops
CHERRY PIE

LIFE

Necco
COW TALES
COW TALES
CHEWY CARAMEL WITH A CREAM CENTER

ALSO ON THE TABLE were several egg cartons; some of these cartons were filled with mini cinnamon rolls topped with pig-shaped candies, and others were filled with mini cupcakes topped with horse-shaped candies. The cupcakes were labeled "Egg Carton Cupcakes" (labels included on the CD). On the front corner of the table was an M&M's candy dispenser that I made with an actual chicken feeder base (purchased at a farm supply store) and a vintage mason jar screwed into the top. Behind the candy dispenser was a small bushel basket that I filled with straw and brown swirl lollipops from my shop. We used Mason jars as drinking glasses for fresh lemonade, and a red-and-white striped paper straw was placed in each jar

IN FRONT OF THE MAIN TABLE was the cutest little vintage tractor. There was a straw wreath embellished with fabric rosettes resting against the tractor's rear wheel. I also put an antique metal milk jug in front of the table and arranged a vintage door and an old pitch fork (both found at an antique shop) off to the side.

A three-tiered metal basket organizer was placed in front of one of the barn doors at the farm. In the top basket were yummy cupcakes adorned with fondant toppers. The corn on the cob–shaped toppers were purchased online from Parker's Flour Patch's online Etsy shop, while the barn-shaped toppers were from www.CookieCovers.net. The middle tier held some old-fashioned candy, including Cow Tails, Chick-O-Sticks, and chocolate Necco® Wafers. The bottom basket was filled with bags of Old-Fashioned Sanded Candy Drops.

I USED A LARGE WOODEN SPOOL to create a second table and set it up next to the duck race station. I covered the top of the spool table in red floral fabric and burlap. Turquoise berry baskets from my shop, lined in red gingham fabric, were filled with scrumptious strawberries.

A CHICKEN-WIRE BASKET was used to display the darling farm animal caramel apples. I made these by sliding a thin wooden dowel through the top of several apples, dipping the apples in caramel, and then coating them in various colors of Wilton Candy Melts®. Before the candy coating hardened, I pressed a fondant farm animal face (made by Marcee of Dippidee) onto the side of each apple. I set an upside-down yellow crate behind the caramel apples for added depth. On top of the crate was a large Mason jar filled with seeds for guests to scoop into some small cotton bags, as another party favor (the template for the seed sign is included on the CD). Another large Mason jar was filled to the brim with red gumballs. I purchased a pair of cowboy boots from the thrift store and spray-painted them a fun aqua color to create unique vases. One of the boot vases was placed next to the gumball jar and the other sat at the bottom of the spool next to a vintage glass jar and a cute farmer's market wall hanging.

ON THE FOOD TABLE, I used a rustic-style cake stand to hold several soup cans tied with ripped fabric strips. Inside each can was an old-fashioned soda, a napkin, a paper straw, and a set of wooden utensils—a simple and cute way for the guests to easily carry all of those items in just one hand, leaving the other hand free for their plate of food. A vintage milk bottle was used to hold extra paper straws, and a painted ceramic boot was put next to the straws.

AT THE END OF THE WATER TROUGH used for duck races, I set up metal rectangles that had the letters S-H-A-N-E painted on them (the birthday boy's name). Next, a thick rope was carefully hot glued onto the side of the metal trough, spelling out E-M-M-A (for the birthday girl). The hot glue was great because it could be applied at a low temperature, making it so it peeled right off after the party.

THE THIRD PARTY TABLE wasn't actually a table at all, but rather was a small wooden wagon! On the front seat of the wagon were brown paper favor bags, dressed up with pennant banners across the tops (made with scrapbook paper, leather cording, and baker's twine from my shop). A cute brown twist lollipop was sticking out of the top of each bag. On the backseat of the wagon was a large antique milk bottle, a framed birthday saying, a small metal milk can filled with red candy sticks, and a small wire basket full of green watermelon gumballs In the center section of the wagon was a cute red-and-white cake stand holding precious farm animal sugar cookies ordered from www.AllThingsExquisite.com. I also found a miniature wooden bench lined with chicken wire and used it as a seat for two rows of yellow marshmallow Peeps®.

REX
PURE LARD
FARM FRESH
ICE CREAM
CHURN STYLE

TEXACO
Unleaded
FARM FRESH
APPLES

ISN'T THE OLD GAS PUMP AWESOME? Once I saw it I knew I wanted to use it as a backdrop for something at the party. Placing the wash basin filled with ice and old-fashioned soda bottles in front of it was perfect for a "fuel-up" station. All the kids loved the fun soda bottles and drank the sugary liquid to their heart's content through fun, striped paper straws.

THE WAGON WHEEL FENCE that surrounded the pavilion at the Staheli Family Farm was the perfect backdrop for the ice cream station. I filled several small Mason jars with strawberry ice cream and secured the screw-top lids on the jars. Then I covered the lids with squares of fun floral fabric and tied it on with red and white baker's twine. I put the cute ice cream jars into an old galvanized canning bucket filled with ice to keep them cool. The template for the ice cream sign that was secured to the bucket is included on the CD.

NEXT TO THE BUCKET was a fun metal chair with a vintage red bucket placed on top. Behind the ice cream bucket was a yellow stool where I set a glass milk bottle which I used as a vase for pretty yellow flowers.

WE HELD THE PARTY at the perfect time of year—spring! Tiny baby rabbits, the farm's newest members, were brought out for the children to hold. They were absolutely precious, and the kids were thrilled to have a chance to pet and snuggle them.

GUESTS WERE INVITED to fill fabric-lined bushel baskets (adorned with fabric rosette flowers) with apples as they left the party. The cute sign used for the Apple Favors is included on the CD.

Do you want to re-create this party?

Combined with the templates on the CD and the party details in this chapter, the list below will give you everything you need to get started!

Farm venue—Staheli Family Farms (www.StaheliFamilyFarm.com)
Invitation, cupcake toppers, labels, signs—Included on CD
Ribbon, small glass milk bottles, lollipops, candy, burlap table cloth, cotton bags, candy sticks, paper straws, wooden utensils, berry baskets, Mason jar drinking glasses, small glass honey jar with spoon, gumballs, Wilton Candy Melts®, napkins, baker's twine, paper shred, scrapbook paper, paper bags—Kara's Party Shop (www.KarasPartyIdeas.com/Shop)
Farm Animal cake pops—Autumn Lynn's Chocolate Sin's Online Shop (www.etsy.com/shop/AutumnLynnsSins)
Barn cake, caramel apple fondant faces—Marcee Kitchen of Dippidee (www.Dippidee.com)
Metal letters, small metal farm truck—Hobby Lobby
Farm Animal sugar cookies—All Things Exquisite online shop (www.AllThingsExquisite.com)
Vintage style drinks and candy—www.CrackerBarrel.com
Corn on the Cob fondant cupcake toppers—Parker's Flour Patch online shop (www.etsy.com/shop/parkersflourpatch)
Barn fondant cupcake toppers—Cookie Covers online shop (www.CookieCovers.net)

EASTON
JONATHAN
EASTON

LITTLE GUY IN A TIE BABY BLESSING OR CHRISTENING LUNCHEON

Photography by Lyndsey Fagerlund

www.LyndseyFagerlund.com

A baby blessing or baptism is a precious event. It's a wonderful occasion for close friends and family members to come together in celebration of one of the family's newest additions. Of course, if people are gathering, it's also a perfect excuse for a party.

WITH SO MANY extended family members and friends invited for the baby blessing of my son Easton, I wanted to make the luncheon following the event both memorable and special. I hoped it would reflect how much I loved my new little baby and also show my appreciation for the support from everyone who came to be a part of his day.

I WENT WITH A LIGHT COLOR SCHEME—mostly whites, very light blue, and pale green. I also wanted to incorporate touches of eyelet & lace into the spread. Finally, I integrated a tie theme so the party could be elegant but not feminine. The whole setting was gorgeous and delicate, just how I hoped it would be.

THE INVITATION was custom-made by PaperAndPigtails.com just for Easton's special day. The design was simple and included blue-and-white stripes, a classic onesie, and a green polka-dot tie. I wrapped a strip of blue patterned fabric around each invitation to add dimension and charm. Once I saw the completed invite, I was inspired to use both the onesie image and the patterned fabric throughout the party.

I PAINTED A VINTAGE DRESSER all white and used it as my main table. I hung eyelet paper lanterns above the dresser and strung a darling banner made of square pennants and eyelet flowers across the front of it. Desserts of all shapes and sizes were arranged carefully on top of the dresser. Cute light-blue-and-green treat boxes were put on both sides of it, so guests could fill them with sweets of their choice.

ON A TALL WHITE CAKE STAND, the main focal point of the dessert display was the precious cake made by Jennifer Hanna, decorated with striped fabric and a fondant circle pennant banner spelling out Easton's name.

ON ONE SIDE OF THE CAKE, I placed delicious key lime cupcakes purchased from Dippidee with fabric pom toppers, and on the other side were margarita cupcakes with tie-themed paper toppers. In front of the cupcakes were pistachio and coconut marshmallow squares, mini white lace cakes, white chocolate and lime cake bites, and adorable tie-shaped sugar cookies.

I USED BOXES covered in white wrapping paper to lift some of the platters, adding height and dimension to the display.

OTHER DESSERTS on the table included white Jordan almonds, white pillow mints, white candy sticks in a delicate eyelet tin, mint French macaroons, white rock candy, vanilla ribbon candy, and key lime truffles. I love using online sources for shopping, especially for desserts! Most of the sweet table items were purchased online and shipped right to my front door! This made the preparation a lot easier since I didn't have to run from one bakery to the next. All of the vendors for these fabulous desserts are listed at the end of this chapter.

ADJACENT TO THE DESSERT TABLE was the food table, which was covered with a custom-made "Little Guy in a Tie" tablecloth. Arranged on the table were gable box lunches. I wanted the lunch aspect of the party to be unique but also easy. It took some preparation to assemble them, but the boxed lunches were a huge hit. And the best part: clean-up was a breeze! Inside each box were a chicken salad croissant, baked pita chips, pasta salad, and a bunch of grapes. The pasta salad was in clear plastic deli containers and the other items were in green or blue striped paper bags. I affixed coordinating labels with the name of each food to the bags and containers so it was easy to know what was inside.

I ALSO AFFIXED a "Menu" label to the outside of each gable box. I used light-green baker's twine to attach wooden spoons, forks, and knives to the top of each box. "Easton" was hand-stamped onto each of the wooden utensils. I prepared separate children's food boxes as well. They included a peanut butter and jelly Uncrustables® sandwich, mandarin oranges, chips, and a drink box.

LIME WATER WAS SERVED both in a glass pitcher and in a tall beverage dispenser. Darling green-and-blue striped paper straws from my shop were placed in another eyelet tin next to the water.

I ABSOLUTELY LOVE ADDING FLOWERS to my parties! No matter what the occasion, they make any celebration more beautiful. I arranged a lovely, all-white spring mix of calla lilies, carnations, and gerbera daisies in a tall rectangular vase and tied a delicate fabric piece around it. The vase was placed on the corner of the food table where everyone could enjoy it.

I PAINTED A VINTAGE HUTCH WHITE, which was a companion to the dresser that held the desserts. I centered the hutch on the back of the food table to both create a backdrop and add a place to display more party elements.

THE HUTCH HELD FRUIT KABOBS, more white rock candy sticks, wooden letters spelling out "Easton," white grapefruit slices, and—most important—cupcake mix favor boxes. I ordered the mixes and favor boxes from the online shop at www.FavorBoxBakery.com, so I would have something to give to guests as they were leaving. The favor boxes had cute coordinating labels on them that read "Easton's Baby Blessing. May 15, 2011. Thank you for sharing this special day with us." Pretty blue ribbon tied the boxes up perfectly.

Do you want to re-create this party?

Combined with the templates on the CD and the party details in this chapter, the list below will give you everything you need to get started!

Glass apothecary jars, mini favor boxes, gable boxes, wooden utensils, rock candy, ribbon candy, pillow mints, Jordan almonds, candy sticks, baker's twine, striped paper straws, clear plastic deli containers, striped paper bags, paper lanterns, flower eyelet garland, ribbon—Kara's Party Shop (www.KarasPartyIdeas.com/Shop)
Cake—Sweeten Your Day Cakes by Jennifer Hanna (www.Etsy.com/Shop/SweetenYourDay)
Invitation and party printable downloads (banner, tags, labels, etc.)—Paper and Pigtails (www.PaperAndPigtails.com)
Cupcakes—Dippidee (www.Dippidee.com)
Tie-Shaped sugar cookies—Bee's Knees Creative (http://www.BeesKneesCreative.com/)
Custom table cloth—Pots & Pins (www.PotsandPins.com)
Key Lime truffles—Truffle Kerfuffle (www.Etsy.com/Shop/TruffleKerfuffle)
Pistachio and coconut marshmallow squares—Oh Yum (www.Etsy.com/Shop/OhYum)
Cake bites—Isabelly's (www.Etsy.com/Shop/Isabellys)
Custom cupcake mix favor boxes—Favor Box Bakery (www.FavorBoxBakery.com)

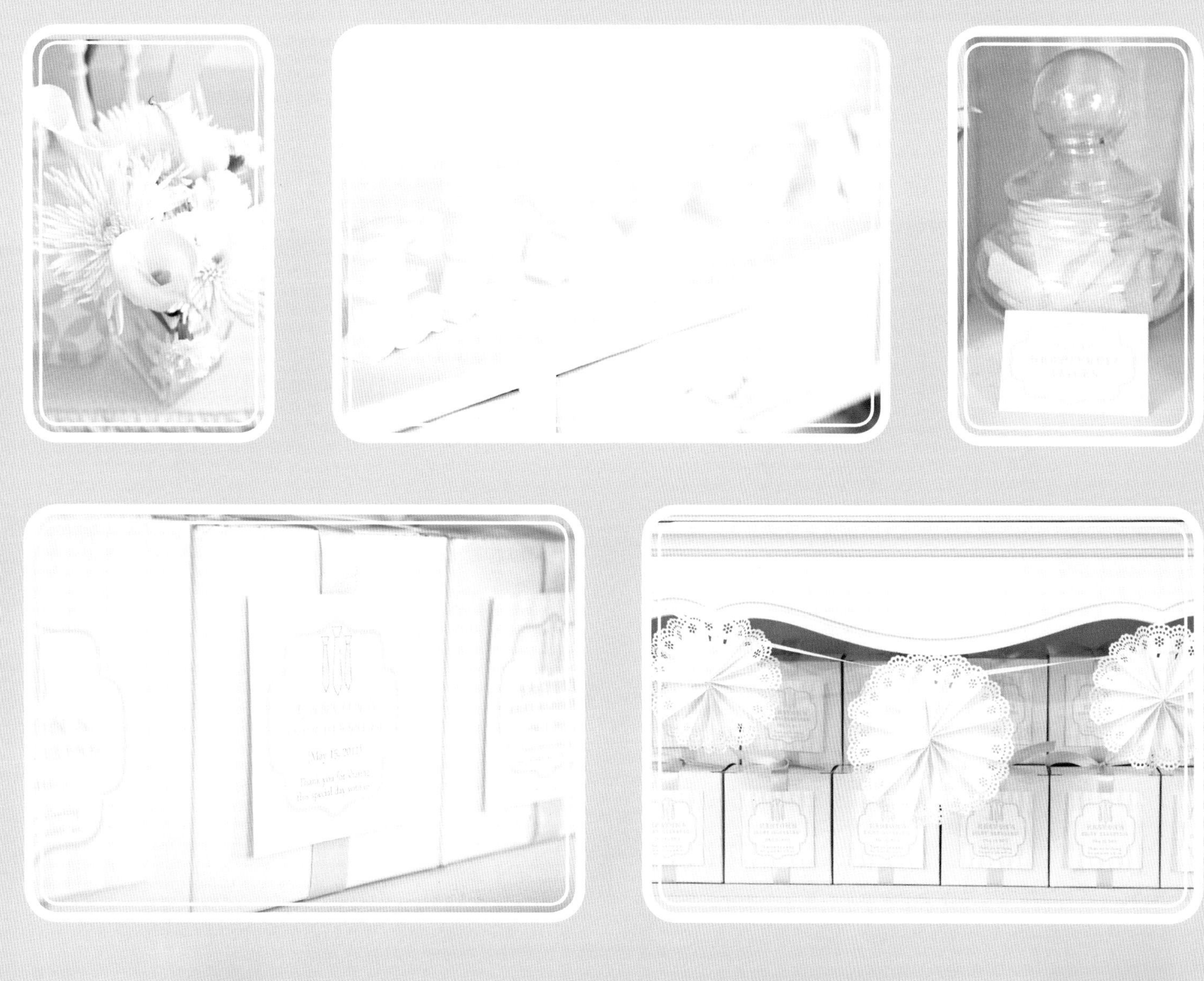

EASTON

ALICE IN WONDERLAND MAD HATTER TEA PARTY

Photography by Valerie Hart Photography

www.ValerieHartPhotography.com

Turn the key and walk through the doorway that will lead you down the rabbit hole. When you get to the bottom, you'll find yourself in the middle of the forest, right in front of a whimsical cottage where a fabulous Mad Hatter Tea Party awaits! It's a topsy-turvy, very merry unbirthday party, and you're invited!

THIS ALICE IN WONDERLAND Tea Party was so much fun to style. From the invitations to the magical cottage location (a small building behind the Strawberry Creek Bakery in Santa Clara, Utah), not a detail was left out. The invitation from the "Fish-Footman" (included on the CD) was designed especially for this celebration. I wanted it to have a dressed-up playing card look, as if it were an invitation from the Queen of Hearts herself.

AS THE GIRLS ARRIVED AT THE PARTY, they were greeted in the center of the clearing by a tall tree with directional signs attached. Each of them was given a frilly skirt, bright leggings, and a whimsical top-hat headband. I bought the headbands online and embellished the felt top hats with an assortment of ribbons, feathers, miniature rabbit ears, birds, and butterflies.

THE GIRLS FELT RIGHT AT HOME in their whimsical outfits amongst all of the dazzling wonderland party accessories. They were also given brightly painted skeleton-key necklaces, made with various ribbons and cording. The girls felt just like Alice and went around imagining that they could open little doors and boxes with their cute key necklaces. They also got sugary candy necklaces with rabbit charms.

THE MAIN TEA PARTY TABLE was bright and bold, decorated in pink, lime green, purple, orange, aqua, and yellow. I placed a striped, lime-green tablecloth underneath a pink-and-white polka-dot tablecloth, which I lined with yellow pom-pom trimming.

THE OBVIOUS MAIN FOCAL POINT of the table was the large teacup centerpiece that I made by painting and embellishing three large ceramic teacups in purple, aqua, and yellow. I stacked the teacups in a topsy-turvy manner on top of a fun yellow hatbox and placed a painted orange doorknob at the base. At the very top of the tower were a Mad Hatter's top hat and a large clock. A small pocket watch hung down the side of the teacups as well.

DRINK
ME

TWO LARGE, OBLONG TEACUPS were placed on either side of the main centerpiece. A blue polka-dot one sat in the basket portion of a pink wire bike, while a green polka dot one was inside a purple wire teacup. I put bright feathers, large glittery mushrooms, silk flowers, mushroom picks, and wire and mesh flowers inside of each of the cups, adding to the fanciful feel.

AT EACH PLACE SETTING was a stack of mismatched plates in all patterns, colors, shapes, and sizes. Small spoons and forks topped with mini painted cupcakes were used as silverware. A dainty teacup with a bendable straw was placed at the top of each setting and included a tag that read "drink me" with a tiny rabbit ear peeking out from behind. These printable tags are available on the included CD. On top of some of the plates were "playing card" cookies (ordered from AllThingsExquisite.com) and little pie slice–shaped treat boxes. The treat containers were filled with toadstool rings from my shop and flower-shaped mini marshmallows. Dreamy butterfly- and flower-shaped wire place card holders displayed adorable playing card–themed place cards (also included on CD) at each child's seat. For more fanciful fun, specialty mini topsy-turvy cakes were ordered from Marcee Kitchen of Dippidee, and each little girl got her own. The cakes were all different colors and sizes and were decorated with delectable frosting forming swirls, polka dots, flowers, and more.

JUMBO CHESS PIECES were also placed around the "mad" tea table. Fun glass teapots and kettles, painted in stripes and bright patterns, were also scattered around.

I FOUND SOME DARLING colored glass bottles that were perfect for the party and put them out on the table. I attached more of the "drink me" tags to their tops. In keeping with the woodland feel, I balanced moss-covered topiary balls on top of candlesticks and staggered them around the two party tables. Ceramic mushrooms were also on the tables, in all sizes and designs.

BUTTERFLY AND TEA KETTLE lollipops were scattered throughout the party—a few were on top of plates, some were sticking out of jars and vases, and others were in various fun places around the party.

A FEW OF THE SMALL wooden chairs were adorned with paper rosette flowers, which were made out of colored card stock and decorated with crepe paper, feathers, ribbons, and tulle netting. Adorable butterfly pillows accented some of the other chairs.

THE BIRTHDAY GIRL sat at the head of the table on a small, pink armchair, perfect for a Mad Hatter's tea party. On her plate was a jumbo spade-shaped trinket box, along with the pie slice–shaped container filled with treats.

A SMALL DESSERT TABLE was displayed atop a white vintage desk, which was set against the front of the cottage. One of the focal points on the dessert table was a clock that I painted hot pink and adorned with a bright blue key secured to the front and a lime green painted crown on the top. I also imagined Alice carrying a basket filled with moss, feathers, flowers, her key, a butterfly, and even the Rabbit's small pocket watch, so I placed the basket on the corner of the desk as if she had accidentally left it there.

IN THE CENTER of the white desk was a cake stand, ornamented with purple metal roses, that held more of the fun topsy-turvy cakes. Delicious meringues were layered on a delicate blue milk-glass cake stand. Darling tea cup–shaped sugar cookies and more playing-card cookies were set on a doll-sized pink metal chair.

10/6

SITTING ON TOP OF A SMALL YELLOW STOOL were scrumptious cupcakes, adorned with Mad Hatter–themed fondant toppers, also made by Marcee Kitchen; the designs included the Cheshire cat, a pocket watch, a green top hat with an invitation on its brim, and wonderland-type flowers and toadstools.

I ALSO SPRUCED UP a small birdcage by painting it bright orange and adding feathers and shiny butterflies to its sides. I made several mini cake stands by gluing wooden candlesticks to wooden discs, and painting them all in bright colors. They were used to hold more of the mini cakes and placed around the table.

THE AMAZINGLY DETAILED CAKE POPS were ordered from the online Etsy shop of Autumn Lynn's Chocolate Sins. I displayed them on a gift box that was shaped like a slice of cake and decorated with pink pom ribbon and rickrack. It served perfectly as a place to showcase the darling cake pops shaped like the Cheshire cat, the Queen of Hearts's crown, the Mad Hatter's top hat, and Tweedle Dee.

TWO WHIMSICAL DOORS were used as a photo op backdrop. I hung a banner that read "A Very Merry Unbirthday" between the edges of the doors. I made the banner by attaching rectangular pennants to pink ribbon and yellow ruffled crepe paper (the pennant template is included on the CD).

HONEYCOMB LANTERNS and fanned paper flowers were hung at either side of the banner, and metal pinwheel yard stakes poked out of the ground. A second banner was strung in front of the doors for an extra splash of color while we took the girls' photos. I made this banner with "tea time" playing cards, ribbon, more honeycomb lanterns, fanned paper flowers, and bright, patterned lanterns. The girls sat on a bench in front of the photo backdrop and posed with different items—such as parasols and "Drink Me" bottles—for a snapshot that was later given to them as a party favor.

Do you want to re-create this party?

Combined with the templates on the CD and the party details in this chapter, the list below will give you everything you need to get started!

Invitation, "Drink Me" tags, place cards, "Unbirthday" banner—Included on CD

Tea cups, butterfly and tea kettle lollipops, pie-shaped containers, crepe paper, honeycomb lanterns, fanned paper tissue flowers, lanterns, place card holders, toadstool rings, cupcake utensils, ribbon, rabbit charm candy necklaces, tulle netting, toadstool picks, miniature rabbit ears, cake piece boxes, Tea Time playing cards, butterfly picks, Mad Hatter top hat, parasols—Kara's Party Shop (www.KarasPartyIdeas.com/Shop)

Alice-themed cake pops—Autumn Lynn's Chocolate Sins online shop (www.etsy.com/shop/AutumnLynnsSins)

Teacup and Playing Card sugar cookies—All Things Exquisite online shop(www.AllThingsExquisite.com)

Fondant cupcake toppers and Topsy-Turvy cakes—Marcee Kitchen of Dippidee (www.Dippidee.com)

Chess pieces, feathers, glass bottles, toadstools, giant tea cups, plates, metal chair, metal bike, directional signs, replica skeleton keys, silk flowers, moss topiaries, metal pinwheels—Hobby Lobby

SKY
AWAY!

HOT AIR BALLOON PARTY

Photography by Valerie Hart Photography

www.ValerieHartPhotography.com

Up, Up, and Away! It's a First Birthday! Since the first year of life always goes by way too fast, a hot air balloon–themed first birthday party based on the phrases "Soaring Through the First Year" and "Up, Up, and Away" seemed very appropriate. The phrases themselves were used throughout the party and were conveyed through various party elements.

THIS PARTY HAS SPECIAL MEANING for me since it was in honor of my youngest son's first birthday. In addition to conveying how fast my baby Easton has grown, a hot air balloon theme also seemed fitting since Easton's birthday is in the spring. Spring is definitely known for being a time to get outside after being indoors all winter, and what better way is there to welcome in spring than with a day at the park flying kites or airplanes or taking a hot air balloon ride! Easton's party obviously had a lot of different hot air balloon elements, but I also incorporated kites and other things that "fly" or "soar" in the sky. I wanted the theme to be something memorable and captivating, a party to celebrate the baby of our family, the boy who, all too soon, will grow up, up, and away.

I CHOSE A COLOR PALETTE of light shades of blue, green, and yellow. I thought these set the tone perfectly for a springtime party. I also added a chevron pattern to the spread, in various coordinating colors. It was a great accent to the geometric shapes of kites and hot air balloons.

THERE WERE SO MANY POSSIBILITIES when it came to decorations for the party. A lot of fun things were used to create a "soaring" feel. The best part of the decor for the party was the printable party pack I purchased online from Leah of www.PrintasticDesignShop.com. Leah did an amazing job of customizing the hot air balloon printables to match my vision, colors, and occasion. Everything was adorable and so easy to print, cut out, and use.

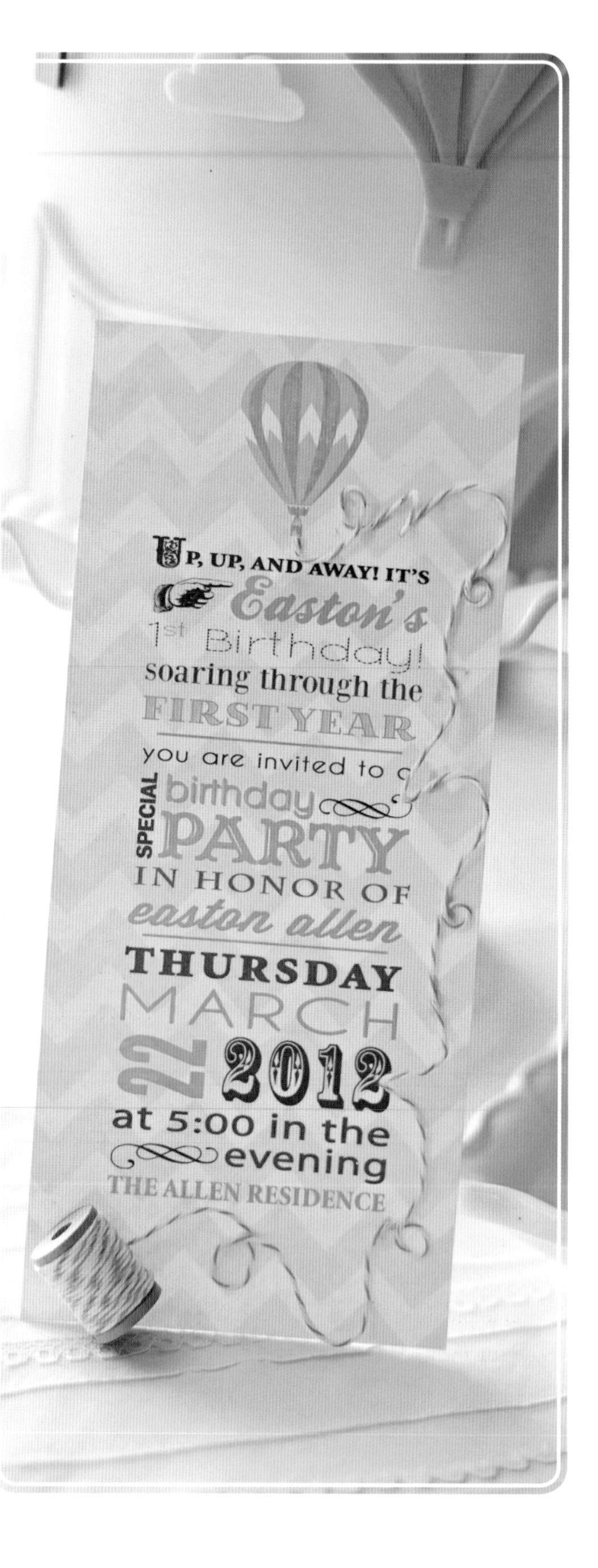

THE INVITATION for the party was just dreamy. It was customized by Leah of Printastic Design and effortlessly printed at home in my office. After the invitations were printed, I glued a small wooden sewing spool wrapped in baker's twine to the bottom portion of each one. I then glued a strand of excess twine along the side of each invite, making a fun swirly design. Finally, I attached the end of the twine just under the top hot air balloon image, creating the look of the balloon being tethered to the spool so it couldn't fly away.

I WOULD HAVE LOVED for the party to be outside, but because of the windy March weather, the party had to be indoors. Breezes may be perfect for flying kites, but they aren't ideal for a party display. I tried to bring the outside in, however, by placing the main party table under a large window in a room near the front of my home. The result was that a lot of light came through the window onto the party table, making it so the sky itself was the ultimate party backdrop. The table was covered in a dainty piece of white fabric adorned with ribbon and lace, which I sewed into a tablecloth. I strung and looped a light aqua ribbon from one side of the front of the tablecloth to the other. I wanted the ribbon to resemble a flying kite string.

I CREATED SOMETHING SPECIAL for guests to sign as they arrived at the party. I do not normally have guests sign something at a birthday party, but since this was Easton's first birthday, and since I came up with an idea that matched the "Up, Up, and Away" theme, I wanted to provide a signature table. I bought a blank canvas at a craft supply store and stamped the bottom of the canvas with a cute bike image. I then drew small upward lines to resemble balloon strings. Each guest made two or three fingerprints on the canvas (if you used this idea for a larger party or wedding I would advise guests to only stamp one fingerprint per person to provide ample room for everyone), and signed the side of one of their fingerprints. The final effect is of balloons flying on strings attached to the bike and it turned out to be just darling. I love the fact that we can treasure it always.

THE CAKE LOOKED GORGEOUS as the main focal point of the table in front of the window. It was inspired by an original cake made by Jessica Harris of Jessi Cakes, and Jennifer Hanna of Sweeten Your Day Cakes did a wonderful job of matching the colors and hot air balloon party theme. It is now one of my most favorite cakes. I just loved the white fondant clouds, the 3-D hot air balloons in yellow and green, and the striped valleys bellow the balloons. The cake was topped with a paper banner from the Printastic party pack (ordered from www.PrintasticDesignShop.com) that read "Easton."

TO HANG IN FRONT and to the side of the main table, I made hot air balloons out of yellow Chinese lanterns, white pom ribbon, paper from the Printastic party pack (folded and made into rosette flowers), grosgrain ribbon, and baskets. They were just precious! I also used the Printastic party pack to make little kites, rosettes, and hot air balloons, which I then glued onto a chipboard letter E. It was further embellished with baker's twine and buttons in coordinating colors. I used a cross-stitch frame to make another dainty hot air balloon decoration. In the center was an image from the Printastic party pack that read, "Soaring through the 1st year" and "Up, up, and away," adorned with another homemade rosette that also resembled a hot air balloon. More baker's twine was attached to the bottom of the frame and a small metal bucket hung as the hot air balloon basket.

THE CHARMING hot air balloon garland hanging above the main table was made out of string, round circles cut from colored cardstock, and painted thimbles.

ANOTHER GARLAND was also created with blue, green, and yellow water balloons—filled with air instead of water—and strung with a medium sized needle onto baker's twine. The garland was simple and really inexpensive, yet added so much to the decor.

TURKEY AND SWISS CHEESE WRAPS were served for lunch, held together with yellow and blue drink stirrers that I used as food picks. The wraps were set out on a green, blue, and yellow striped serving tray. I hand stamped solid yellow and green-and-blue striped napkins with a hot air balloon stamp and set them next to the sandwiches. Make sure to use ink that won't rub off onto your guests! Water bottles were dressed up with labels from the Printastic party pack, wrapped with baker's twine for a delicate touch, and placed in a light-blue basket. Next to the basket were small drink boxes wrapped in hot air balloon–print paper, for the little ones. This is such a cute way to spruce up inexpensive drink boxes. Simply pull off the straws and wrap the small boxes like you would a gift. Punch a hole in the top part of the paper, directly over the straw hole (but not through the foil of the drink box) and reattach the plastic-wrapped straw to the back of the box with a glue dot or tape.

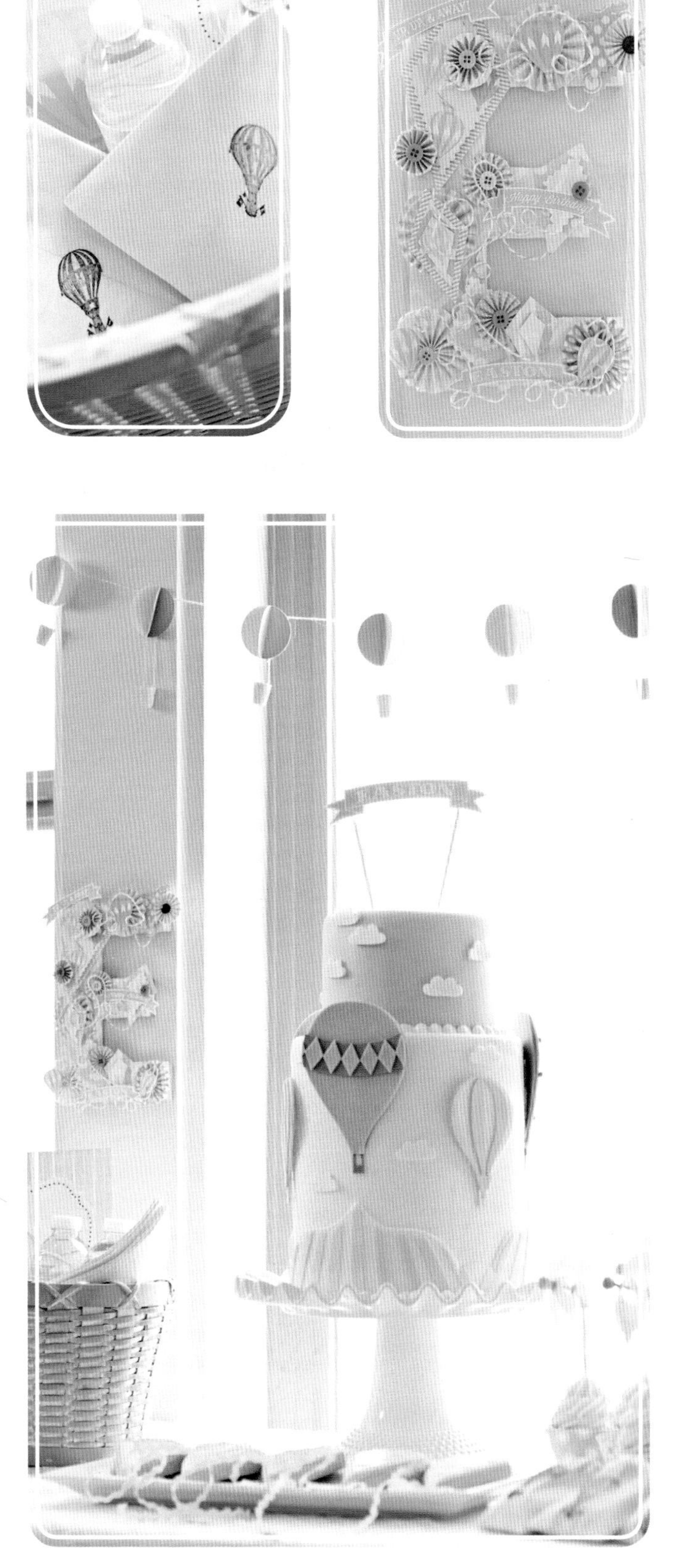

AWAY!

SKY
Limit!
AWAY!
birthday

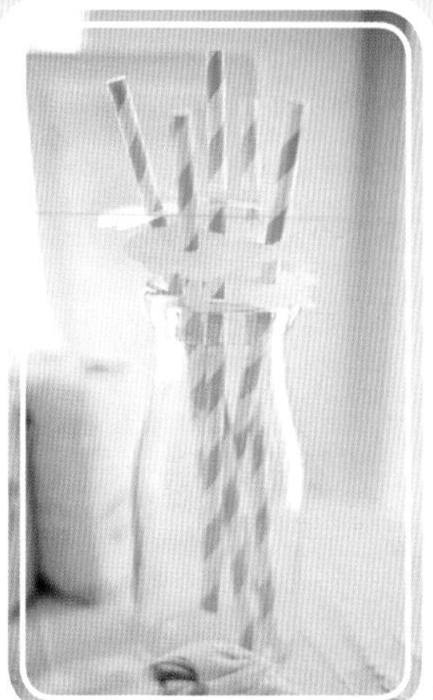

NEXT TO THE DRINKS were yellow-striped paper straws sticking through fun clouds that were cut out from the Printastic party pack. I arranged the straws in a small glass milk bottle. The stunning hot air balloon cookies, ordered online from Jen of www.AllThingsExquisite.com, were laid out on a rectangular ceramic plate, which was lined with some of the chevron paper from the Printastic party pack. Jen never ceases to amaze me; her cookies are always perfect and taste just as good as they look! She also created the adorable kite cookies, which I likewise placed on a rectangular ceramic plate. I carefully laid a piece of aqua rickrack (accented with a bow) underneath the bottom of each kite as the kite strings. Jen also made the white, cloud-shaped cookies, which were actually displayed upright on wooden dowels in a clear rectangular dish filled with rock candy.

ANOTHER CLEAR RECTANGULAR DISH held the heavenly hot air balloon cake pops, ordered online from Autumn Lynn's Chocolate Sins. They were just precious and were a favorite among guests. Lemon bars from Flour Girls & Dough Boys in American Fork, Utah, were beautifully enhanced with chevron print fondant toppers ordered from the Etsy shop of Parker's Flour Patch. The lemon bars were carefully placed on an ornate, white square platter. They didn't last long; guests ate the treats as fast as they were put out. The other desserts that were well loved were the splendid vanilla and lemon cupcakes from Dippidee. I inserted cupcake toppers, made using the Printastic party pack and my circle paper punch, into the top of the vanilla cupcakes, and wrapped them in cupcake wraps, also from the Printastic party pack. The topped cupcakes were displayed on a light green hobnail cake stand. The lemon cupcakes were also wrapped in the printable cupcake wrappers, but instead of the circle toppers, they were adorned with small white pinwheels.

CUTE MINIATURE PLASTIC PARFAIT DISHES from my shop were filled with vanilla pudding, which was covered in whipping cream and topped with darling paper banner images from the Printastic party pack. Next to the pudding were small plastic cups filled with blue raspberry Jello® topped with whipped cream.

RESTING ON THE JELLO® CUPS were mini clear plastic spoons from my shop. Paper envelope-type treat bags in various designs and prints from the paper party pack were filled with light cotton candy. A tent card, also from the party pack, was placed in front of the envelopes that read "Cotton Candy Clouds."

WE ARE FORTUNATE to have so many of our family and friends live nearby, so the party included a lot more guests than a typical first birthday party might. An extra chocolate cake purchased at my local wholesale warehouse was dressed up with a miniature pom banner strung from yellow-and-white striped paper straws. I have seen many poms made with yarn, but I wanted these to be dainty and thin, so I used baker's twine to make them instead. This particular pom banner has become so popular that I presented a tutorial on how to make it on one of my TV episodes on www.MyCraftChannel.com/shows.

FOR PARTY FAVORS, I filled clear pillow boxes with light blue M&M's and decorated each box with a round printable tag from the Printastic party pack. I found some small plastic baskets at a craft supply store, which I thought looked just like hot air balloon baskets. The pillow boxes were placed inside of the baskets and displayed on the table in front of the cloud cookie pops. I also hand-stamped small linen drawstring bags with a hot air balloon stamp and filled the bags with blue rock candy strings. They looked absolutely charming laid out with all of the desserts and decor. Two glass milk bottles were used to hold darling blue-and-white candy sticks that had paper flags wrapped around the tops (made from the Printastic party pack). For additional take-home favors, guests put the candy sticks, as well as other party items like the white pinwheels, into aqua-and-white paper chevron-print bags.

A DAINTY UPRIGHT WHITE FRAME from my shop displayed one of my favorite images from Leah's Printastic party pack—two hot air balloons in front of a fluffy white cloud. The image was framed with blue ornate lines and stripes, surrounded by yellow-and-white chevron stripes.

THE PLACE SETTINGS had two white ceramic plates topped with a blue-and-white striped paper plate. Kite cookies and other yummy desserts were placed on and to the side of each plate, and a small white bucket filled with white paper shred and more M&M's was put in the center of each plate. I tied some baker's twine to the buckets and attached a yellow balloon filled with helium to each one to create a "flying hot air balloon" effect. Many more helium-filled balloons lined the tall ceiling of the room. At the end of each balloon string was an adorable paper tag made using the Printastic party pack. Each fun tag had a coordinating saying or image on it.

EASTON'S HIGH CHAIR was decorated from top to bottom with themed elements. I made two long pinwheels using balloon sticks and pinwheel downloads from the Printastic party pack and attached them to the top corners of the highchair.

STRUNG BETWEEN THE PINWHEELS was a banner that read "Up &." The rest of the banner was attached to the high chair tray and read "Away!" The paper pennants that were used to make the banner were cut out from the Printastic party pack and glued to some cute yellow grosgrain ribbon. Behind Easton's high chair, I hung a large piece of aqua-and-white chevron-print fabric. The colors looked so good together.

EASTON HAD A BALL dabbing at and finally digging into his blue-frosted vanilla smash cake covered in white fondant clouds. The precious smash cake was also made by Jennifer Hanna of Sweeten Your Day Cakes..

Do you want to re-create this party?

Combined with the templates on the CD and the party details in this chapter, the list below will give you everything you need to get started!

Invitation, signs, decorated paper, cupcake toppers and liners, paper banners, tent cards, cotton candy envelopes, paper tags, ribbon banner images, water bottle labels, paper pinwheels—Customized Printable Party Pack from Leah Barrus's online shop, Printastic Designs (www.PrintasticDesignShop.com)

Ribbon, bike and hot air balloon stamps, baker's twine, rickrack ribbon, paper straws, pillow boxes, chevron paper sacks, glass milk bottles, paper shred, rock candy, plastic parfait cups, miniature plastic spoons, napkins, striped paper plates, Chinese lanterns, upright white frame, sucker sticks, linen drawstring bags, circle paper punch (used to cut out tags and labels), balloons, napkins, cardstock, miniature metal buckets, glass jars, M&M's, baskets, chevron print paper bags, water balloons—Kara's Party Shop (www.KarasPartyIdeas.com/Shop)

Large two-tiered cake and smash cake—Sweeten Your Day Cakes by Jennifer Hanna (www.Etsy.com/Shop/SweetenYourDay), inspired by an original cake made by Jessi Cakes (www.JessiCakesBlog.blogspot.com)

Cupcakes—Dippidee (www.Dippidee.com)

Hot Air Balloon cake pops—Autumn Lynn's Chocolate Sins online shop (www.etsy.com/shop/AutumnLynnsSins)

Hot Air Balloon cookies, cloud cookie pops, kite cookies—All Things Exquisite online shop (www.AllThingsExquisite.com)

Pom cake topper banner tutorial and other party tutorials—Kara's Party Ideas—The Show (www.MyCraftChannel.com/Shows/)

Chevron fondant cookie toppers—Parkers Flour Patch online shop (www.etsy.com/shop/parkersflourpatch)

Lemon bars—Flour Girls & Dough Boys (www.FlourGirlsAndDoughBoys.com)

UP&
UP, UP & AWAY!

UP&
AWAY!

Easton
Easton

Thank You

First and foremost, I want to say thank you to my wonderful husband and best friend, Ben. Without you, none of this would have happened. Thank you for your unending love and tolerance of my brain being full of nothing but party ideas during all of this. Thank you for playing both dad and mom during the countless hours of work. I don't deserve you. Your words of encouragement and sweet kisses are what lifted me up and kept me going when I knew the countless hours of work had just begun.

Mom, you have taught me so much. I'm doing all of this because of you and for you. I don't know how you raised us four kids on your own. You are one amazing woman and are nothing but selfless. I can't even remember you ever taking time out for yourself. You always stayed positive, even when you didn't know what the next day would bring or how you were going to do it. That has taught me more than you will ever know. I promised myself over and over when I was a little girl that when I grew up I would do everything in my power to help you finally have the life you deserve. It's my turn now, and your turn to stop worrying. I will not give up.

Grandpa and Grandma Slaydon, you have been my second set of parents. What sweet examples of dedication and kindness you have been. I love the two of you more than words can say. Thank you from the bottom of my heart for ALL you have done for me.

Amber Pugmire, where do I even begin? You are unequivocally irreplaceable. I can't even fathom the countless hours you put into this book. You sacrificed so much, and in so doing, your family also sacrificed so much. Thank you for being so supportive, and for being my number one cheerleader. Thank you for always knowing just what to say and just what I need. You are more than an assistant; you are a best friend.

Jamie Moffitt, when I think of the word "friend," I see your face. You dropped everything and came to my aid over and over. You drove the hour distance between your home and mine through snowy blizzards and pouring rain just to help a stressed friend. It meant more than you will ever know.

Brynne Louder, I will always look back and remember the great talks and good laughs we had (I don't think I have ever laughed so hard). You were the one who could outlast the rest on the no-sleep scale. You know how night owl gals like ourselves work. Thank you for helping me for hours on end with all the photo shoot preparations. Those were some good times, and, as crazy as they were, I will miss them greatly.

Kimberlee and Travis White, thank you for helping so much with my boys. They adore the two of you. Thank you for being so willing to help wherever there was need!

Dad, thank you for your wonderful example of how to just get in there and work. I have your work ethic in me, which I couldn't have done any of this without. I keep going and going and *going* because of watching you do the same throughout my life. We both can't ever sit still! I also function on little sleep thanks to your genes! You are a wonderful man and I am proud to call you my father.

Larry and Darla Allen, I don't know how I lucked out with such amazing in-laws. From the first time I met the two of you, you took me in like I had been your daughter from the get-go. Thank you so much for your support. You have done so much for me, and I love you dearly.

Kaden, Gavin, and Easton, Mommy loves you to the moon. Being your mom has brought me more joy than life itself. I feel so blessed to have such sweet and tender souls as children. Thank you for teaching me so much with your innocence and purity. I want you to know that you can live your dreams. I will be your number-one fan in all that you do.

To the rest of my family and friends, how could I forget you? You have ALL been my support army and I wish I could list you all by name (that would take a whole other book). Grandma Wilford, Grandma Fern, Great-Grandma Slaydon, aunts, uncles, cousins, youth leaders, bishops, teachers, friends—thank you for believing in me. Thank you for your wonderful examples, and thank you for molding me into the person I am today.

Thank you so much to the beautiful children who attended and modeled at these parties. And for your sweet mama's for being so patient with me and my team! Aspen Osmond, Andelyn Osmond, Jake Mizukawa, Ashley Mizukawa, Makayla Mizukawa, Adelin Olsen, Easton Olsen, Brindee Heaton, Abigail Ostler, Sophie Ostler, Ty Slade, Bridger Blackher, Halle Church, Sadie Church, Emily Church, Brecken Harrington, Taylor Harrington, Hallie Harrington, Lydia Jo Moffitt, Logan Moffitt, Brigham Hart, Stockton Hart, Kaitlyn Ringwood, Jackson Pugmire, Hadleigh Pugmire, Emma Smith, Owen McCubbins, Olivia McCubbins, Caden Louder, Brigham Louder, Kaden Allen, Gavin Allen, Easton Allen.

Kelli Ostler, you are amazing at finding anything and everything when it comes to shopping! Thanks for being a great friend and for following your heart and coming into my life when I needed it most. I look at you and see the greatest mom, the kind of mom that I want to strive to be daily.

Lizabeth Rolfson, you are an absolute gem. Thank you so much for putting my visions and ideas into real-life designs and party printables. You worked so hard and did so much for me with such a willing heart.

Valerie Hart and Lyndsey Fagerlund, without your amazing images this book wouldn't stand a chance! You both deserve a HUGE "thank you." I'm very proud to call you my photographers. You both deserve all the credit in the world. I know you will do big things. Keep climbing!

My dearest regards to the team at Cedar Fort, especially Jennifer Fielding, Michelle Stoll, Erica Dixon, and Laura Jorgensen. Thank you for being behind me and for believing in my book. You made this dream become a reality. You have been wonderful to work with and I so appreciate all that you have done!

A huge thank-you to all of the vendors (please see the vendor list at the end of each chapter) who donated so much of their talent and time to this book. I have loved getting to know you, and I appreciate you so much!

Fans and readers, YOU are what keep me alive in all of this. You excite me and motivate me to move mountains. Without you, there wouldn't be any of this. Thank you for following me on this journey. And thank you for your unending love and support. Your emails, messages, gifts, and letters mean so much.

XOXO,

Kara